Preparing Teachers for Urban Schools

Lessons from Thirty Years of School Reform

Preparing Teachers
for Urban Schools

Lessons from Thirty Years of School Reform

Lois Weiner

Teachers College, Columbia University
New York and London

Published by Teachers College Press, 1234 Amsterdam Avenue
New York, NY 10027

Library of Congress Cataloging-in-Publication Data

Weiner, Lois.
    Preparing teachers for urban schools : lessons from thirty years
of school reform / Lois Weiner.
      p.   cm.
    Includes bibliographical references (p.) and index.
    ISBN 0-8077-3251-6. — ISBN 0-8077-3250-8 (pbk.)
    1. Urban education — United States.   2. Teachers — Training of-
-United States.   3. Socially handicapped children — Education — United
States.   4. Teaching — Social aspects.   I. Title.
LC5101.W45   1993
370.71'0973 — dc20   93-4540

ISBN 0-8077-3251-6
ISBN 0-8077-3250-8 (pbk.)

Printed on acid-free paper

Manufactured in the United States of America

99 98 97 96 95 94 93   7 6 5 4 3 2 1

This work is dedicated to my parents,
George and Gladys Weiner,
who taught me the importance of helping others;

to my husband, Michael Seitz,
who assisted me in every way he could
during my research and writing;

and to the memory of Dick Broadhead,
who inspired me to teach and organize.

6/11/96

Contents

Foreword

For over a century and a half in the United States, the central, unyielding dilemma in teacher education, baldly stated, has been: Does a professional program prepare bright, motivated, and idealistic teacher-novices for the way things are in classrooms now or prepare them to teach in classrooms the way they ought to be? In *Preparing Teachers for Urban Schools*, Lois Weiner examines that dilemma and others that have persisted over the last three decades in institutions committed to preparing the next generation of teachers to work in big city schools. She details an unpleasant story of neglect, indifference, and confusion. Her analysis, fortunately, does not leave readers floundering in pessimism, but offers us constructive alternatives for designing urban education programs.

Weiner's central point is that most well-intentioned urban teacher-education programs (including such federal efforts as the Teacher Corps and Training Teachers of Teachers) have continually concentrated on children and teachers' deficits rather than focusing on how city schools, as bureaucratic institutions, have helped shape work conditions that prevent effective teaching and on building communities of interest among teachers, parents, and children. Her recounting of the history of such stigmatizing labels as "culturally deprived," "inner city children," and "at risk" provides compelling evidence of the "linguistic denials" joined in by too many teacher educators, researchers, and policy makers.

Weiner argues convincingly for more attention to the school ecology within which children's actions, teachers' behaviors, and school performance are intertwined. The institutional setting of most big city schools, she points out through personal anecdote and numerous data, sets the boundaries for both teaching and learning. For teacher education programs to ignore such matters in lieu of targeting teachers' behaviors or students' shortcomings invites further charges of irrelevance.

She argues persuasively that preparation programs for urban teachers must avoid the "teacher/scholar" model of the Master of Arts in Teaching (M.A.T.) efforts of the mid-1950s and 1960s and the mistakes of the 1960s and later in concentrating on teacher and student deficits. Instead, programs must help novices work through the inexorable dilemmas of dealing with individual differences in a bureaucratic institution; how to focus on and use students' cultural and class differences in teaching while developing a sense of classroom community and respect for a larger culture; and how to synthesize the inevitable differences between practice and theory. These tension-filled dilemmas are deeply embedded in urban education programs and won't go away. Weiner describes them vividly, making sure that readers understand the core issues with which university educators and new teachers must wrestle.

Weiner has written a book that is informative, jarring in its analysis of prevailing assumptions about preparing urban teachers, and constructive in its designs for improved programs. She has not lost her idealism. She knows that new teachers' energy, spirit, and determination to improve the lives of their students are precious resources; and rather than have them erode or evaporate—as research studies document—they must be conserved and transformed into diamond-like strength that will persist past their first enervating year in an urban school.

The passion that infuses this book is credible to me. It rings of insider knowledge. Weiner's experiences as a teacher and teacher educator recreate the smell, tang, and feel of teaching in public schools. She knows well the dilemmas of both teacher education and the joys and difficulties of daily teaching. Few books on teacher education carry such authority of experience, blending analysis and passion, as this one does. There are no easy solutions here. I am uncertain whether what Weiner proposes can be done. But I do know that it is worth trying.

Larry Cuban

Introduction

This text examines the problem of preparing teachers of at-risk students in urban schools. The topic contains two entangled threads: the issues raised in teaching disadvantaged students and the problems of teaching in an urban school system. The strands represent, perhaps in quintessential form, teaching's features as a calling and as a job: An ideal of helping poor, minority students frequently motivates people to work with disadvantaged students; yet urban teachers perform within a system that constrains them from addressing these students' needs. The urban teacher's ideal of service must be maintained in conditions that subvert fulfillment of that goal, generating an unrelenting conflict for teachers of at-risk students in urban schools.

The conceptual framework I have used has been shaped by 20 years of teaching, reflection, and union activity, punctuated by periods of research. Because my conceptual framework is the instrument I use for analyzing the scholarship of the past 30 years, a brief explanation of the attitudes and experiences that have formed it is in order.

The broad political thesis underlying my research is that to fulfill human potential, we need a society that has the widest and most popular forms of political freedom and economic democracy. The aim is inseparable from the means used to attain it, so no elite—benevolent or despotic—can bestow it. When people act together in conscious struggles against injustice and inequality they change conditions and themselves. Their activity helps to illuminate alternative social, political, and economic arrangements that sketch the ways in which society could be organized.

Frequently when people who experience injustice struggle as a group against the conditions they find insufferable, they do not recognize all the implications of their struggle, and their actions may be inconsistent with their professed aim of freedom from injustice. For example, labor unions in this country have a tragic history of complicity with racist, exclusionary employment practices that have kept black workers and women in the least lucrative jobs. Or in another instance, the civil rights movement failed to allow the fullest participation of female activists within its ranks, a process that encouraged women to form their own organizations and movement. What makes these movements progressive, and worthy of support, is their struggle to democratize aspects of social, political, economic arrangements.

Though people who are denied the opportunity to fulfill their potential do not always recognize a commonality of interest, I think all these movements share a goal that cannot be achieved by a single movement, or at another's expense. Their goals cannot be met unless social and economic relations are utterly transformed, and that process will take a sustained, vigorous struggle by all who recognize the inequality and injustice of the status quo.[1]

These political ideas were at the heart of my decision to teach, but in addition I reasoned that teaching would be socially useful, give me considerable autonomy, and allow me to achieve a modest level of material comfort. I was greatly influenced by Richard Broadhead, a political co-thinker and friend who enjoyed his work as an elementary school teacher but derived more satisfaction from leading the Berkeley Federation of Teachers. Dick saw no moral or political conflict between his teaching and union work, and believed that teacher unionism was the most promising vehicle for improving schools, so long as the union earned the trust and support of parents and community members. His concomitant beliefs, that more fundamental economic and political change was necessary, that education could not solve many of the problems that reformers attributed to poor schools, did not diminish his resolve about organizing a progressive teacher union movement that would challenge the status quo on behalf of teachers, parents, and students.

Teaching meant union activity, and it was this component, not the work with children, that initially gave me the sense of purpose that makes many people think of teaching as a calling. Only after I had taught for a few years did I develop the great affection for adolescents and the involvement in subject matter that draw many people to teaching.

The political ideas and commitments that motivated me to become a teacher have changed little in the past 20 years, but my teaching experiences and graduate study have deepened my understanding of the interplay between politics and pedagogy. As I read more in philosophy and history of education, I learned that I admired and agreed with John Dewey's work, from his involvement with early efforts to build a teachers' union, to his writing on curriculum and teaching. Dewey's understanding of the educative value of experience corresponded to my own political thinking and developing pedagogical philosophy: Freedom, like knowledge, must be gained through activity; political struggles are educative because the activity transforms one's understanding of the world as it is and as it might be. In a similar vein, the most effective learning occurs when students work toward an outcome that is valuable to them and connected to their life experience.

My premise, that teaching is both a calling and a job, and that both are legitimate concerns, is not a universally accepted viewpoint. Clearly, my commitment to teacher unionism and my political thinking about the ways in which life circumstances, social and economic, influence our behavior laid the groundwork for appreciating the ways that urban school characteristics constrain urban teachers' performance. Similarly, my ideas about teacher unionism's broad social responsibilities have made me gravitate to a framework of urban school reform that makes parents, teachers, and community members partners in change. The specific topic of this work was prompted by my teaching experiences in the New York City schools and in three other school systems.

After teaching high school successfully for seven years in three markedly different suburban systems, I began work in Julia Richman High School, which is typical of most of New York City's neighborhood high schools. More than 3,000 students were enrolled, most of them children of working class and poor Hispanic and black families from East Harlem. I had taught in a large multiracial, working class high school in Hayward, California, a small high school in a wealthy community (Bedford Hills) in suburban New York, and in Malverne, a bedroom suburb on Long Island that had experienced serious racial conflicts in its schools. I was an experienced, mature, confident teacher when I started teaching in New York City; but I felt inadequate and disoriented, unprepared and frightened in my first term teaching at Julia Richman.

Like most large urban school systems, New York retains the same vocabulary and operations it adopted at the turn of the century. Because most of the teachers are themselves products of the New York City schools, the procedures and lingo are familiar to them, but not to a stranger. Duplicating machines are called "rexographs," not "dittos" as they are everywhere else; teachers (until 1990) punched time clocks and when they were transferred involuntarily to another school were "excessed." Classroom teachers take attendance on small white "Delaney cards" which fit into slotted cardboard pages in a "Delaney book" and are collected after each term. The old wooden chairs and desks in my classroom were bolted to the floor, and all supplies had been ordered in March for September.

Previously I had taught students from minority and immigrant groups, and I had enjoyed working with students who had poor academic skills, choosing to teach remedial reading and writing courses. However, nothing in my academic preparation or classroom practice had prepared me for this typical New York City high school. For example, I was given a homeroom of more than 40 ninth graders and was expected to perform several clerical jobs, most important, taking attendance, within ten minutes, although most students arrived at homeroom late. Attendance had to be taken in two ways, hand-recorded with arcane symbols in a notebook and also with computer punch cards. A colleague in a neighboring room advised me to lock the door after the late bell, marking students absent who were not in their seats on time. Although I felt this was draconian, in my desperation I adopted her suggestion — until one of her enraged students set fire to her classroom door after being denied admission.

Almost a year elapsed before I regained confidence in my ability. In the next seven years, in two other New York City high schools, I came to enjoy my students more than I had any others in my career and to savor their energy, wit, and savvy. They, administrators, and my colleagues acknowledged that I was a superior teacher when I was named "Teacher of the Year" by the WestSide Chamber of Commerce. When I decided to use what I had learned in my teaching career to prepare prospective teachers, I enrolled in a doctoral program at Harvard Graduate School of Education. At Harvard I had the opportunity to rethink my transition to urban teaching and to examine scholarship on urban teacher preparation. Why did I experience so much difficulty in adapting to the New York City school? Why had I been able to make the adjustment? My difficulties during that year prompted my interest in this study as my doctoral dissertation.

My early research revealed that my preparation to teach had included the standard approaches to learning to teach disadvantaged students, but they had not been effective. In fact, one widely accepted measure, an early field experience, which for me was a semester spent observing and assisting in a racially segregated urban high school, had such a negative impact that I ruled out teaching in an urban school system as my first job. I felt alienated from the students, unable to experience a personal connection between us. Though I had no problem exercising my authority, I did not enjoy the interactions between us and felt that we could not communicate, which, in fact, we did not. For example, on one occasion I led the students in a discussion of what we would call the school newspaper we were going to produce. "What it is!" one student shouted. I responded, "That's what we're trying to decide, what the name is." Other students shouted out, frustrated, "No, no, no! What it is!" After much of the same back and forth, I realized that "What it is" was a slang expression they wanted to use for a title. Most of my interactions with them lingered at this level of miscommunication.

On the other hand, I enjoyed and excelled in my semester of student teaching at an integrated high school in Oakland, but the trauma of my early experience convinced me that I should not immediately pursue a career teaching in an urban high school. Clearly, something was missing from my preparation — and the scholarship that had informed it.

My experience raised another question about teaching poor, minority students. In other settings I had been a well-regarded teacher of students termed "disadvantaged" in much scholarship. Why had I felt so disoriented working with these students in a New York City classroom? My preliminary research pointed to a crucial flaw in most scholarship: Researchers used "inner city" and "urban" synonymously with "disadvantaged," "deprived," or "at risk" to describe poor, minority students. My experience suggested that the characteristics of the school setting (urban or inner city) were a separate problem from the academic characteristics of the students (at risk, deprived, or disadvantaged).

In my first term at Julia Richman I was exhausted and confused by conflicting demands, only some of them due to students' needs. Bureaucratic regulations, like taking attendance with two different methods, combined with inadequate resources to make helping individual students almost impossible. My trauma in homeroom each day illustrated the problem well.

Like most urban school systems, New York's schools suffer from vast truancy, which parallels and predicts its dropout rates. The crusade to improve school attendance is carried out in good part by exerting pressure on teachers to record attendance correctly. During my first semester, I struggled to learn and comply with elaborate regulations about taking attendance in homeroom, in the face of students' understandable anxiety about my recording their presence accurately, even if they zoomed into class 30 seconds before homeroom ended. My homeroom's large size, students' inconsistent attendance, and the assorted clerical tasks that had to be accomplished in the ten-minute period made learning their names a Herculean task. And without knowing their names, taking roll was more difficult.

From talking to colleagues I gathered many suggestions, but most of them did not fit my teaching values. I did not want to assign students seats by their last names because homeroom was the only time besides lunch when they could socialize with friends; I could not in good conscience adopt a policy of marking them absent when they came into the room while I still had the ability to change the record. I could not violate the regulations that prohibited having students assist with taking roll, but I learned that I was, legally, allowed to have a student take the book to the attendance office.

By the second term I had devised a system that allowed me to record attendance and complete other clerical duties, as well as to find out why students arrived late and counsel and cajole them about coming on time. During the first week, I'd ask them to choose a seat, which would be a permanent assignment. I made a seating chart based on their selections, and I warned that in order to take roll accurately, I would wait until the last five minutes, giving them five minutes grace. Once the book left the room in the hands of the student who volunteered to take it to the office, I could make no changes. Developing this procedure freed me to become acquainted with some of my students, which is, ironically, one of the ostensible purposes of homeroom.

This pattern characterized my acclimation to teaching in a New York City high school: I could not enjoy my students until I surmounted the obstacles placed in our path by bureaucratic regulations and lack of resources. As I read research about the characteristics of successful teachers of at-risk students, I recalled dozens of situations in which school regulations and conditions had influenced my interactions with students. Yet, seldom were these kinds of factors considered in teacher preparation, and even more surprisingly, they were ignored in literature on urban school reform.

Although my book takes as its starting point the controversies prompted by the civil rights movement's focus on improving education for black children, it is helpful to understand that preparing urban teachers of poor and working class children is not a new concern. Indeed, the problem of educating children of the cities' lower classes has been discussed since the inception of mass public schooling, as has the issue of educating urban teachers.

A report issued by the federal government in 1914 described how all but one city with a population of 300,000 or more maintained a normal or training school for teachers, as part of the public school system. Most new urban teachers came from the graduating classes of these city training schools.

Although these training schools were run by the school systems themselves, urban educators debated many of the issues that are addressed in contemporary reforms, for example, whether practice teaching should be done within the training school or the regular school setting. St. Louis had the student practice, then return to the training school to "reorganize her work on the basis of the problems teaching has opened."[2] Trenton, on the other hand, had students who had completed their coursework practice teach in regular schools with classes for troublesome students as well as "foreign pupils."[3]

The currently fashionable proposals for university-sponsored "professional development schools" in urban schools attempt to end the institutional polarization that began when state normal schools, later to expand into state colleges, and the city training schools diverged in their judgment about whether the state normal schools could adequately prepare city teachers. Only eight cities relied on state normal schools rather than establishing their own training schools; but in these eight cities the school districts had "no relation to the state school" except to employ its graduates as teachers. The one exception was Providence, which had an agreement with the Rhode Island Normal School to select cooperating teachers, called "critic" teachers.[4] The Providence schools paid the teachers' entire salary and then were partially reimbursed by the Rhode Island Normal School.

Do urban teachers of at-risk students require special preparation, and if so, who can best provide it? This question prompted much research during the 1960s and 1970s, and most of it ignored the fact that the issue first arose with the creation of the state normal schools and was hotly debated at the time. For example, in comparing advantages and disadvantages of city and state training schools, the Superintendent of Newark argued that the state normal schools needed to adapt their training methods when educating city teachers. He observed that usually a state graduate required

> a longer time to "find" herself in a city school system — or for that matter, in a rural school district; her knowledge is too general; it is not specific enough to meet special cases. The correction to this is much practice work before being graduated.[5]

Contemporary proposals to reform teacher preparation have ignored this history, as well as scholarship of the recent past. As Larry Cuban noted in his critique of the Holmes Group report,

> There was a federally funded effort to revitalize teacher education, invigorate urban teaching through conceptualizing a different role for teachers, and alter schooling for poor children and those of color. Tens of thousands of teachers were trained in schools across the country.

> Thousands of university faculty enlisted. Scores of research reports
> and studies were written. . . . The absence of references to previous
> relevant, large-scale programs to point out earlier flaws in conception,
> execution, or institutional barriers suggests a long-term memory loss.[6]

Cuban's criticism of the Holmes Group's historic amnesia applies to
the other major teacher reform proposals of the 1990s, which fail to
acknowledge or learn from two decades of research and debate about
how best to educate teachers of poor, minority children. One aim of
this book, then, is to ameliorate the historic amnesia of current reform
efforts, that is, to analyze the problem of preparing urban teachers of
at-risk students in light of previous attempts.

The two most influential reports, by the Holmes Group and the
Carnegie Task Force on Teaching as a Profession, share an assumption
that "the key to success" in reforming American schools "lies in creating
a [teaching] profession equal to the task."[7] As Gary Sykes observed, the
premise that teachers and, in turn, teacher preparation can serve as an
effective mechanism for educational reform underlies most new efforts
to improve schooling.

> The current reform wave rightfully places the teacher at the heart
> of what is known as "educational excellence." . . . In all the states,
> however, governors, legislators, and business and educational leaders
> are focusing on the improvement of teaching as a critical element —
> perhaps *the* critical element — in the promotion of educational excel-
> lence.[8]

However, teacher education may not be "an effective mechanism
for educational reform," as one important study concluded 20 years
ago.[9] Use of teacher preparation to reform schools is untenable, Larry
Cuban has argued, because "fundamental alterations in schools are
linked to political changes outside schools" and "basic changes in the
[schools'] organizational structures are necessary prior steps in any sustained effort to touch what teachers do daily in classrooms."[10] What is
the appropriate relationship between teacher preparation and efforts
to improve the education of disadvantaged students in urban schools?
In Chapter 5 I explain why teacher preparation can make modest improvements in the ways people teach, but that it cannot reform schools,
as many teacher preparation programs have demanded.

In arguing that teacher preparation is a legitimate vehicle for improving the instruction that poor, minority students receive in urban
schools, this book adopts a perspective on school reform that is associ-

ated with James Comer's "ecological" and Don Davies's "holistic" approaches. I share Comer and Davies's assumption that the school and community must be linked and that school *systems* must be altered because systems, not isolated factors, subvert academic achievement.[11] As I discuss much more fully in Chapter 5, Comer has criticized the educational reforms of the 1960s for their uncoordinated foci on children's families, teaching methods, and classroom organization, rather than on the "quality of relationships between home and school, among staff, and between staff and students and the effect of these relationships on school learning."[12] Davies makes a similar criticism of most efforts to improve the education of disadvantaged children: They fix blame on one of the parties and arrive at solutions that fasten on only one element of the child's world.[13]

I have adopted the "ecological" or "holistic" perspective because it best expresses my belief that schooling must take into account all of the child's life experiences and that education's psychological and sociological demands are inextricably connected, as Dewey argued. Comer is a psychiatrist and Dewey was a philosopher, but in their approach to school reform both take as a starting point the child's psychological needs, arguing that they can be fulfilled only by addressing the child's social needs and society's demands. Although Comer's school reform efforts initially did not call for the kinds of educational practices usually associated with Dewey, Comer eventually saw that child-centered strategies were the only ones consistent with his goals.

In recognizing that a child's psychological development and educational growth occur most fruitfully in a setting that draws on family and community strengths, Comer has placed himself squarely on the side of social scientists who have argued that schools must change to adapt to their students, rather than vice versa. On the other hand, Comer also argues that schools must meet the needs of all who are part of the school community and that schools cannot be improved by attacking a single factor, or at the expense of one constituency. With these ideas he separates himself from the bevy of educational researchers and reformers who have pinned the blame for academic failure on some single factor or constituency: parents, teachers, administrators, curricula, culture.

Comer's approach to improving schooling for poor, minority children exemplifies Dewey's commitment to expanding democracy by encouraging common struggle to make the school a democratic community. Thus I have adopted Comer's perspective in my analysis of the research on urban teacher preparation, and I have identified an underlying conceptual flaw in much of the scholarship of the past 30 years.

Material on preparing teachers of disadvantaged students in urban schools has generally focused on *either* the attributes of disadvantaged students and their teachers *or* the demands made on teachers by conditions in urban schools. By using "inner city" as a euphemism in describing poor children of color, educators have encouraged confusion about two wholly different issues, the demands of the setting and the needs of the children. The description is demographically accurate because urban areas have the greatest concentrations of students described as "disadvantaged," but the terminology has obscured a critical conceptual flaw in discussions of urban teacher preparation. The issues of student characteristics and school setting are interwoven but not identical, and the use of "urban" or "inner city" to describe students has muddled discussion of both topics and obscured the relationship between them.

Scholarship in the social sciences has confirmed that the urban school setting shapes student and teacher performance. Yet, for the most part, discussion of urban teacher preparation has ignored this work and remains fixed on identifying characteristics of teachers and students, completely divorced from the school context. Using the work of sociologists, anthropologists, political scientists, and historians in a study of urban teacher preparation shifts the traditional focus on individual student and teacher attributes to a broader portrait of schooling that includes analysis of problems generally excluded, like funding and school regulations. This expanded perspective provides an escape from what has proven to be an educational dead-end: the search to explain poor, minority students' school failure in terms of either student or teacher characteristics. In adding another dimension to Comer's "holistic" perspective, this study locates the issue of how best to prepare teachers of at-risk students in urban schools within what Daniel Liston and Kenneth Zeichner, among others, describe as the "social context of schooling."[14]

A vast amount of material has been written about the topics addressed in this work, too much, it may seem, for one work to synthesize. According to one estimate, more than 200 colleges and universities sponsored special programs to prepare teachers for the disadvantaged in 1971.[15] Unfortunately, much of the research is seriously flawed, in design or methodology, and it does not require detailed examination. In addition, this study is not an exhaustive analysis of the literature within the topics discussed, but rather an examination of their *intersection*, the ways in which the topics have influenced each other historically and the way their intersection should inform reconceptualization of teacher preparation for at-risk students in urban schools.

Another reason this study was feasible despite the considerable quantity of material is that educational discourse frequently reflects major political debates of the times. Research about the broader social and political context in which the discourse occurred has made the material amenable to categorization, by identifying major strands in the debate. The danger of this method is that it can produce an overly schematic analysis which overlooks subtle but vital differences among advocates of similar ideas. As a safeguard I have made every effort to examine points of view that do *not* conform to the either/or formulations that seem to delineate public debate.

In the first three chapters I examine four closely related questions and the answers given them in the past 30 years. First, what have researchers identified as the skills and attitudes teachers of at-risk youth in urban schools need to be successful? Second, how should teacher preparation be changed to give teachers these skills and attitudes? Third, how do characteristics of urban school systems affect teacher and student performance? Finally, how should teacher educators use an understanding of these characteristics in devising programs of urban teacher preparation?

I should explain why this study looks at characteristics of urban school *systems*, not individual schools. A wealth of scholarship demonstrates that urban school systems share distinguishing characteristics, and first-person accounts of the way systemic conditions in urban schools, like large classes and heavy teaching loads, alter teacher performance have corroborated historical studies and many of my personal observations. Limiting the study to characteristics of urban systems is not meant to suggest that conditions are identical in all urban schools within the same system or that urban and nonurban systems do not share common problems. On the contrary, schools can respond differently to the conditions imposed by their systems, as the effective schools research indicates, and both urban and suburban school systems suffer from many common problems. Precisely because schools may adapt differently to the same restraints, this book examines the characteristics of urban school *systems* as they affect teacher preparation.

Chapter 4 summarizes the history of research on preparing teachers of at-risk students in urban schools, placing the research in the context of contemporary efforts to reform schools and teacher preparation. Chapter 5 analyzes how teacher education might improve education for at-risk students in urban school systems and explains why a holistic approach to school reform is needed. Chapter 6 makes recommendations for the kind of preparation that teachers of at-risk students in urban schools require. I have been fortunate in having had the opportunity, in my current role as a faculty member in the teacher preparation program at Jersey City State College, to test the ideas I advance in the final two chapters. As I discuss in detail in Chapter 6, my thinking has been enriched by my work with colleagues and our students to prepare prospective teachers for urban schools, the challenge our department and school have taken up.

Debate about how best to prepare teachers of poor, minority students has been politically explosive since the civil rights movement made educational opportunity a central policy issue. In this work I have tried to convey my understanding of the political issues underlying scholarly disagreements, as well as advance my own point of view. However, I have attempted to discuss these highly charged concerns in a polite but forthright manner, acknowledging that thoughtful readers may disagree.

Other readers may be disappointed by the absence of prescriptions for recruiting and preparing urban teachers. I have purposefully refrained from detailing components of a generic program that could or should be replicated. One of the most important conclusions I have drawn from examining scholarship on this topic is that teacher educators have generally failed to take into account the ways in which the gender, race, and social class of teacher candidates influence the kind of preparation they require and receive. The biases of class and gender embedded in elementary and secondary schooling are no less present in teacher preparation but are more often ignored. Even scholars who aptly describe the ways working class and poor students are affected by tracking tend to overlook the "tracks" separating teacher candidates in research universities and those in state teachers colleges. There can be no one best system for educating urban teachers, just as there can be no one best system for educating urban students. The starting point must be a holistic approach, but beyond that each successful program will be unique and will rely on the strengths of its faculty and students.

Rather than proposing prescriptions ("teachers of at-risk students should demonstrate the ability to do x, y, and z") I describe how programs should deal with the disparate needs of teacher candidates, for instance, the particular problems of teacher candidates who have themselves been in lower tracks or those who have always been in elite educational settings. I draw on Dewey's thinking to suggest strategies to assist prospective urban teachers to adjust to the demands of teaching at-risk students. What is most important in this discussion is not the proposals themselves, for many are already in use, but the analysis of why certain strategies are more effective with particular teacher candidates when they prepare to teach in urban schools.

I am indebted to Michael Fultz, who suggested the historical orientation for this study, Roland Barth, whose extraordinarily conscientious assistance as my adviser at Harvard enabled me to complete my research with dispatch, and my husband, Michael Seitz, who subordinated his own writing to the demands I made while completing this project. Brian Ellerbeck, my editor at Teachers College Press, made many astute, well-informed suggestions which have, I think, significantly improved this work. Sadly, Dick Broadhead, the person who prompted me to become a teacher and set me on my present intellectual and pedagogical course, died some years ago. However, I hope his love of teaching and passionate dedication to teacher unionism are communicated in this book, as they were to me 20 years ago.

The 1960s: Educating the "Culturally Deprived Child"

As the civil rights movement of the 1950s and 1960s sparked attention to the educational needs of disadvantaged minority children, researchers began to investigate what schools, teachers, and students needed to boost the academic achievement of poor, minority students in the nation's cities. Spurred by political ideals and increased government and private spending, educators generally addressed the problem in one of two ways. Either they focused on the classroom interaction between disadvantaged students and their teachers, or they examined the demands made on teachers by conditions in urban schools. Thus research from the 1960s is grouped into these two major categories. While these categories are useful in analyzing research during this period, it is important to understand that the writers themselves did not construct these divisions and that not every program and author can be neatly categorized in one or the other.

TEACHING DISADVANTAGED YOUNGSTERS

The solutions arrived at by analysts who emphasized the problem of teaching disadvantaged students apart from the issues raised by the urban school setting depended on how disadvantagement was defined. When it was defined as an intellectual or cultural deficiency of the student, the family, or social class, as it was in Project TRUE, a program of Hunter College to assist first-year teachers in New York City junior high schools, the teacher needed an "awareness of the deficits of the children,"[1] an understanding that "lower class children are often anxious or compulsive or both"[2] and lack the "conventional experience, language facility, emotional security, self-confidence, and self-control of middle class children."[3] In *The Challenge of Incompetence and Poverty*, J. McVicker Hunt, an educator, explained that the poor, whether black or white, typically do an "inadequate job of teaching their children the abilities and motives needed to cope with schooling, even though they love their children as much as any parents do."[4] When the problem of disadvantagement was thus described, teachers needed to be familiar with students' "incompetence" and able to assist their charges in overcoming linguistic, behavioral, and cognitive deficiencies. Successfully teaching disadvantaged children also required the ability to "achieve a sense of success and worth" from the task, which was difficult because of the children's problems.[5]

Frank Riessman's work *The Culturally Deprived Child* described the difficulty of educating lower class children. He identified the problem primarily as deriving from conflict between the culture of the school and that of the family. In describing the family culture, he argued that schooling must adapt to the students' culture and "while there may be aspects of the culture" of lower class children that "would be better changed," the educator should "work within the framework of the culture as it exists," except for challenging its "anti-intellectualism," which defeated one of schooling's primary social purposes.[6] He explained that the school should be pluralistic enough to find a place for a variety of mental styles, and therefore the effective teacher would face value conflicts. One solution was for teachers to focus on skills that students wanted and needed; another answer was to acknowledge the disagreements but attempt to change the negative characteristics of the students' culture, like bigotry and anti-intellectualism, "within a framework of general acceptance."[7] Riessman argued that the culture of the educationally deprived students demanded teachers capable of establishing unvarying routines in classes, with clear, enforced rules built around the goal of learning; acknowledging past difficulties; and encouraging the possibility of future success.

Although he entitled his study *The Culturally Deprived Child*, Riessman criticized labeling disadvantaged students as "culturally deprived" since, he argued, lower socioeconomic groups possess a culture of their own different from that of the middle class. Riessman proposed the term "educationally deprived" to describe and define the problem: the students' limited access to education. Three of the four reasons Riessman gave for academic failure derived from the school's inability to adapt to the students' culture; only one related to deficits in the students' family and class culture. Further, Riessman stated that the segment of the population that is most disorganized by the social environment, that which might actually be called culturally deprived, is relatively small and therefore examining it can tell us little about how to educate the mass of poorer children.

Thirteen years later, James Comer made a similar observation:

Black families who managed to adapt socially and psychologically to economic deprivation differed from those who did not. He noted that this important differentiation received little attention in analyses and reforms in the 1960s.

> We too often lumped all black students together. We often failed to identify their different aspirations, strengths and weaknesses. Most important, we ignored the alienation — and often open anger — between home and school.[8]

Riessman's insistence on the importance of understanding, respecting, and accepting educationally deprived students' culture and adapting schools to the students' culture differentiated his work from much other writing of the period. However, two reports commissioned for the University of Missouri Trainers of Teacher Trainers reflected Riessman's concerns. One report stated that teachers of disadvantaged students needed to know that "their condition is, in many respects, not a universal one" and that "the valuing game" which occurred in education had certain assumptions that produced "educationally dysfunctional conclusions."[9] A companion study on linguistics contended that a teacher needed subject matter competency, the ability to understand the child's conceptual state, and the ability to mediate between these two tasks; in addition, the teacher's role as a "classroom organiser within a larger, complex organization" also needed consideration in determining the essential skills and attitudes for teaching children who were not middle class.[10] These attempts to locate the teacher–student relationship within a larger context of school and society were the exceptions. Most of the literature, like the work by Hunt cited earlier, fixed responsibility for poverty and educational failure on student deficiencies. The terminology for describing students from poor, minority families who did not achieve success in school changed from "culturally deprived" to "disadvantaged," but the definition of "disadvantagement" remained strikingly like that of "cultural deprivation." For instance, *Education of the Disadvantaged* used "disadvantaged" and not "culturally deprived" to describe students from lower-income families, but nonetheless advised school workers that homes of disadvantaged students did not stress "behavioral assets such as obedience, punctuality, cleanliness, and care of personal property" and children were not afforded "much experience with organized group behavior or verbally stimulating tasks."[11]

   The shift in nomenclature coincided with a theoretical challenge to the concept of cultural deprivation, with pointed criticism of the idea that culture itself was the primary cause of poverty or students' educational failure. It was a "bitter irony," one author argued, that the concept of culture, which was borrowed from social scientists to illuminate the ways social conditions rather than innate propensities led to differences in group behaviors, was being used "in a form almost as pernicious in its application as biological determinist and racist views have been in the past."[12] To describe students as "deprived" implied that before starting their education, they had suffered a loss; "disadvantaged" allowed the possibility that students' lack of academic success had causes external to the student or family. Deprivation means loss or privation, that is, the absence of "that which is needed; want of a necessity or necessities," while disadvantaged denotes "loss of advantage."[13] Students who are culturally deprived lack the cultural essentials for success; those who are disadvantaged do not have a privilege that others enjoy.

The conflict between educators who attributed failure in school to the students' culture and those who challenged this explanation was well illustrated in *Education of the Disadvantaged*. One author cited IQ test scores to demonstrate that the disadvantaged student was "not able to cope with the kinds of verbal and abstract behavior which the school demands."[14] Martin Deutsch explained the role of social class in language development and cognition, arguing that lower class children were subject to a "cumulative deficit phenomenon" occurring between grades 1 and 5.[15] However, another author dismissed theories of deprivation, contending that the schools used the family and the community as scapegoats for their lack of effectiveness and that social science defined the problem in such a way as to defend schooling's failures.[16] One selection defended neither perspective but instead identified several strengths of the inner city child; but in their preface to this chapter the editors warned that "lower class positives" might not compensate for the "real deficits slum children bring with them."[17]

Critics of the "culture of poverty" challenged the design and interpretation of research that identified poor, minority students as deficient in their ability to abstract and to develop verbally.[18] An alternative explanation for educational failure was the clash of values between teachers and their clients, either as a result of class differences between lower class students and middle class teachers, or because of other teacher attributes, for instance, age or gender.[19] One author explained that most teachers, while conscientious, were "too middle class, too insensitive, or too fragile to reach ghetto children successfully."[20] The teacher personality "appears to suffer from anxiety, insecurity, submissiveness, fear, and doubts about the fundamentals of democracy," a 1968 doctoral dissertation at Harvard Graduate School of Education explained.[21]

When the cause of student failure was located in a cultural clash

between student and teacher, teachers needed a "conceptual understanding of teaching the disadvantaged" and knowledge of the "milieu
in which these youth grow up."[22] When attributes could not be taught
or acquired, the solution was to attract a different kind of person to
teaching and to "replace the authoritarian teacher" with one who
would nourish talent and individuality.[23]

Paul Goodman, in an aside about the cultural clash between teachers and students, corrected the terminology used to describe the conflict. He wrote that critics who faulted teachers and schools for imposing middle class values on poor children had mistakenly labeled the
school's values, which in the elementary schools were not at all middle
class but rather petit-bourgeois: bureaucratic, time-serving, and timid.
The upper grades and university "exude a cynicism that belongs to
rotten aristocrats," he argued. Rarely communicated is the bourgeois
value of learning that is "truly practical, to enlighten experience, give
courage to initiate change, reform the state, deepen personal and social
peace."[24]

Some material suggested there was "no satisfactory answer" to the
question of whether a "unique set of personal characteristics and competences are necessary for success as a teacher in a disadvantaged area
school," as a report issued by the California State Department of Education concluded.[25] The report's author suggested that a partial answer
might be found in the extent to which the students' needs differed
from those of children considered "advantaged" and that the population
labeled "disadvantaged" was not a homogeneous group but could be
divided by learning styles. Furthermore, the greater the congruity between a child's learning style and the characteristics of the program in
which he or she was required to perform, the greater the likelihood of
school success. Conversely, school failure ensued from a greater discrep-
ancy between the characteristics of student and program. The teacher's
ability to mediate this relationship depended on his or her ability to
personalize instruction and the proportion of students whose learning
styles diverged radically from the program's expectations.

Furno and Kidd concluded that the question of whether teaching
the disadvantaged involved special skills was one of education's "issues
without answers."[26] They suggested no blueprint, "just a groping toward new institutional forms and practices" to meet the changing beliefs, needs, and expectations of citizens, but like the California report
they focused on the teacher–pupil relationship as the key to effective
teaching.[27] In evaluating their four-year teacher education project in a
Baltimore slum, they noted that "high scholarship and its concomitant
interests and attitudes" were not essential for teachers of disadvantaged

children and that a more critical factor was empathetic concern based on actual experience, not preconceived ideas.[28] Still, teachers could not by themselves counteract other factors that affected student achievement, a finding they noted James Coleman had advanced in his 1966 study, *Equality of Educational Opportunity.*

To summarize, posing the question, "What skills and attitudes are needed to successfully teach disadvantaged students?" suggests a prescription. However, seeking a definitive list of skills and attitudes in the literature is fruitless because authors disagreed on the nature, indeed the existence, of "disadvantagement" as a relevant factor in student achievement. Advocates of theories of cultural deprivation identified specific skills and techniques that would allow students to compensate for their cognitive and verbal deficiencies. Authors who attributed students' lack of achievement to a clash between teacher attributes and student values insisted that teachers above all must be knowledgeable and empathetic about the students' milieu; knowledge of specific teaching skills was of secondary importance.

TEACHING IN URBAN SCHOOL SYSTEMS

The teacher attributes and culture of poverty theories focused on the characteristics of and interaction between teachers and students to analyze the skills and attitudes needed to teach disadvantaged students. However, another segment of the literature located responsibility for academic failure on schooling in general and urban school structures more specifically. This portion of the literature can be divided into a "change agent" segment and what I will label a "school structures" analysis.

Change agent material defined the primary task of urban teachers as sparking school reform as individuals.[29] For many proponents of the change agent strategy, teaching had to attract a different kind of person, one with more impressive "personal qualities,"[30] a different type of college graduate "bent on reform,"[31] one who was young and vigorous.[32] Urban teachers were second-rate in an occupation that to begin with attracted less inquisitive, scholarly, and aggressive personnel, argued one author.[33] Excellent urban teachers were "sadly outnumbered by ineffective, unconcerned, and ill-prepared persons occupying space in classrooms."[34]

However, over time the change agent literature became more ambiguous about the extent to which special skills, as opposed to political or personal attitudes, were necessary. For instance, a progress report on the Teacher Corps, a federal program that I will analyze in detail later, observed that teachers needed skills as well as enthusiasm.[35] As the importance attached to teaching skill grew, criticism of teachers diminished. One Teacher Corps instructor noted that many of the change agents who entered teaching in the 1960s in inner city schools left "shaken and disillusioned" because they had only good intentions and didn't realize what skill and work were needed to create the kind of classroom environment they advocated.[36] Another explanation for the increasingly muted criticism of teachers within the change agent literature was that the change agents clashed with veteran teachers in early programs. Some Teacher Corps projects "were wiped out as outraged teachers literally kicked the [Teacher Corps] interns and their carpet-baggers out of their schools."[37]

In general, the skills and attitudes identified for successful urban teaching differed according to the aspects of urban schooling pinpointed for change agent attention, with curriculum, teacher attitudes, and school organization three dominant concerns.[38] Idealism and determination also characterized the successful urban teacher: One teacher educator explained that teacher change agents needed to eschew any "long-range personal commitment" to the ghetto school because that dulled "the chances of radical reform" by "accentuating the positive aspects of struggling and triumphing in what is undoubtedly a nonviable role."[39]

Not all the literature that focused on the urban school as a cause of student and teacher failure advocated that individual teachers spark institutional change. Authors who can be grouped into the second, school structures category attributed disadvantaged students' lack of academic success almost exclusively to the urban school structure. These educators advocated that teachers support newly organized teachers' unions as the vehicle for educational reform. This analysis also suggested that no teaching skills and attitudes possessed by urban teachers could prevail against the limitations imposed by school conditions. An article in the first issue of *The Urban Review* illustrated this analysis: It hailed teachers in New York City schools as "heroes and heroines of endurance" for resisting the infantilization of the school structure and commended "their great union, the United Federation of Teachers," for assisting them in resisting infantilization.[40] Disavowing the teacher attributes explanation for students' academic failure, this perspective faulted school structures, not teachers' middle class origins, for teachers' lack of effectiveness. On the contrary, the teacher "wants her pupils to make good in the sense she understands best — academically."[41]

The emphasis on urban schooling's systemic problems sometimes fused with confidence about teacher unionism's role in educational and political reform to suggest that the most critical skill or attitude for an urban teacher to possess was to be a union supporter. A Harlem principal, featured in a *New Yorker* profile for his school's outstanding achievements, stated that for urban teachers, joining the teachers union should come before encouraging the liveliness of students. He reasoned that with the protection afforded teachers by a union, they could be vital in "advising, participating in and stirring up community action . . . about problems that directly concern the children as well as their parents."[42]

USING TEACHER PREPARATION TO MAKE URBAN TEACHERS MORE SUCCESSFUL WITH DISADVANTAGED STUDENTS

Teacher educators writing during this period disagreed about whether teachers of disadvantaged youngsters in urban schools required specialized preparation. The division was between advocates of a totally revamped system of teacher education and proponents of more limited reform of preparation of teachers of disadvantaged students. Both proponents of theories of cultural deprivation and the critics who argued that teacher attributes caused student failure tended to agree that teaching disadvantaged youngsters required specialized preparation, though in the first case the preparation was designed to assist teachers to adapt to student deficiencies and in the second situation it was to correct deficiencies of the teachers themselves. The authors who found fault with schooling or teacher education in general, among them the change agent advocates, argued for a substantially different system of teacher education to improve preparation of teachers of disadvantaged students, along with the training of all others.

In *Preparing to Teach the Disadvantaged* John O'Brian argued that traditional teacher training programs were doing "an outstanding job of preparing teachers to work with students identified with middle class culture" but these teachers were not prepared for the task of working with disadvantaged youngsters.[43] A special empathy was needed to "understand and appreciate the special needs" of disadvantaged students.[44] O'Brian described a master's degree program designed specifically to prepare teachers of disadvantaged students, noting that an effective program had to contain an interdisciplinary mix of all behavioral sciences and extensive experience in the milieu of the disadvantaged student to sensitize teacher candidates to the world of disadvantaged youngsters, which was so different from their own middle class experience. Similarly, the teacher educators who developed the BRIDGE Project at Queens College recommended specialized preparation of teachers for schools in culturally deprived neighborhoods. They suggested that teacher candidates needed special instruction in methods of teaching educationally disadvantaged children: more time devoted to effective use of audiovisual equipment; instruction in teaching reading to older children; and practice in developing materials with the disadvantaged child in mind. In addition, the project developers recommended that part of student teaching should be in depressed areas.[45]

However, the opposite conclusion was reached by the Task Force of the National Institute for Advanced Study in Teaching Disadvantaged Youth, a project established in 1966 by Title XI of the National Defense Education Act.[46] As the Task Force members studied the problem of preparing teachers for the disadvantaged, they came to "attribute failures and inadequacies of education for the disadvantaged to defects in education of teachers" generally and outlined a plan "to prepare teachers for all children, regardless of their cultural backgrounds or social origins."[47] The Task Force rejected theories that labeled students "culturally disadvantaged" as "denigrating their evolved culture" and "racist," insisting that "teachers must be trained to respect the potential strengths of the disadvantaged" rather than taught "mythologies" that discouraged investment in education.[48]

The Task Force disputed what it called the "false image" of the disadvantaged child, including the idea that all were alike.[49] Given the heterogeneity of U.S. society, a teacher who was able to work with the children of one social stratum or group was inadequately prepared to teach in the common school, the report explained. Furthermore, the problem of training teachers for schools in disadvantaged areas was not the same as the problem of preparing teachers to deal with racism in schools and society. This latter issue was a matter of concern for teacher education generally, since teacher education should lead to an examination of the teacher's own prejudices, as well as an understanding of the problems and concerns of students and parents.

The controversy extended beyond presentation of educational theory to teacher candidates, to the appropriate type of preparation in the teacher's subject area. The Task Force report was adamant that "to specify the subject matter preparation of teachers of the disadvantaged is to indicate the preparation needed by all teachers."[50] In contrast, the BRIDGE Project recommended special English methods classes "to emphasize work with the uninterested and disenchanted child" so that teacher candidates can "become acquainted with adolescent literature that is particularly appropriate for these children."[51]

The bulk of the Task Force report was a detailed plan for an overhaul of teacher education. The only discussion about preparing teachers for disadvantaged students was indirect, in a portion of the report that analyzed why teachers in such great proportions left "deprived areas."[52] The report observed that they leave because, like their students, "they fail." They failed because of their inferior status and their working conditions, which were not described. Three problems in the training of teachers for deprived areas were enumerated: Teachers were unfamiliar with the community and particular conduct problems of students; teachers were unaware of their own prejudices and values; teachers lacked preparation in skills needed to perform effectively.

The Task Force faulted two major innovations in teacher education during this period, the Teacher Corps and M.A.T. (Master of Arts in Teaching), along with traditional teacher preparation programs, for their disregard for theory. These programs, the Task Force argued, taught theory "apart from the realities teachers meet" and gave the student teacher "little theoretical understanding of the situations he meets."[53] They failed to provide a sustained practice schedule of "performance-feedback-correction . . . until desirable skillfulness is achieved."[54] Though the Task Force distanced itself from the reforms attempted by the Teacher Corps, they shared a conceptual consensus that defects in teacher education generally were responsible for the deficiencies in urban teacher preparation.

In explicitly rejecting theories of cultural deprivation, the Task Force attributed the academic failure of disadvantaged students to flaws in contemporary schooling per se: "There is little excitement in the school for anyone: the poorer one is, the drearier his school experience."[55] The report explained that teachers generally confused racial, class, and ethnic bias with academic standards, especially in the study of language. But most critical to the reform of teacher education was an understanding that people had such difficulty coping with depersonalization, that a teacher first of all had to be human, able to win students' trust.

Nowhere, however, did the Task Force address how its proposed overhaul of all teacher preparation would address these problems. How would teachers become familiar with the conduct problems of students in deprived areas? And how were these problems different from those faced by teachers of underprivileged students? Although the report explicitly rejected the concept of "cultural deprivation," it offered no alternative explanation for classroom management problems faced by teachers of students in deprived areas.

Describing the assumptions of the Cardozo Teacher Corps Project,

Larry Cuban echoed most of the Task Force criticisms of education. Like the Task Force, Cuban contended that low-income youngsters had the same general needs and values as those with more advantages, and that similarities outweighed any differences in behavior. Similarly, teachers, regardless of race, could make a difference with low-income children, but what defeated teachers of those youngsters was the conventional teacher role. The "teacher-dominated, text-bound, student-recitation" class "has failed to stimulate or educate," he explained.[56] He argued against applying generalizations about poor and minority students because teachers "must deal with groups but treat members as individuals."[57] He rejected the explanations for student failure that depicted disadvantaged students in terms of middle class white children and schools.

The Task Force recommendations for reform of teacher education and solutions offered by change agent advocates were shaped by differing estimations of the role of teacher preparation in improving education for the disadvantaged. The Task Force outlined methods to improve the quality of teaching generally but proposed no specific connection between these reforms and improved schools for the disadvantaged. Most advocates of reform through a change agent strategy, especially the early Teacher Corps personnel, viewed reform of teacher education as the primary vehicle for improving education for the disadvantaged, contending that a superior teacher candidate who received superior preparation could successfully spark overall improvement in schooling.[58] This emphasis on the individual teacher's role encouraged a critical view of veteran urban teachers, as well as a focus on school conditions needing reform, especially developing and using appropriate curricula and materials.

Cuban's description of the Cardozo Teacher Corps Project in Washington, DC illustrated both characteristics. Cuban argued that schools trapped teachers and other school staff into behaving as people who didn't like children, and that both inexperienced and veteran inner city teachers suffered from a "spastic rigidity" that was reinforced by an accidental convergence of institutional pressures and teacher education truths.[59] Their personal rigidity and academic blinders were reinforced by conditions within the schools, such as their isolation, class loads, clerical duties, and multiple preparations. In its attempt to describe the connection between urban school conditions and teachers' interactions with students, Cuban's 1970 study was one of the rare works in the literature of the period to treat both issues and their interrelationship. However, Cuban did not explain the connections he identified between teachers' inadequacies in classroom practice and institutional pressures, nor did he analyze the cause of the institutional problems he described.

Not all the proponents of using teacher education to spark reform in urban schools and of making newly trained teachers change agents concurred with the negative assessment of teachers that characterized much of the change agent analysis. Faith Dunne, in "Survival of the Innovative Teacher: Preparing Liberal Arts Graduates to Work for Change in the Public Schools," faulted many M.A.T. programs that had "fostered a sense of elitism and . . . failed to induce sensitivity to the needs and expectations of traditionally trained teachers, or to their potential areas of common concern."[60] Dunne contended that the change agent concept was itself sound, but that M.A.T. programs utilizing it were so flawed that enrollees were given neither an accurate sense of the culture and social relations in urban schools nor the techniques to survive and to effect change.

In conclusion, just as scholars in this period provided no prescription for the attributes of successful teachers in urban schools, they produced no answer to the problem of reform of teacher education because there was no consensus about the nature of the problem. Confounding the basic problem of defining disadvantagement was disagreement about whether urban school conditions required special preparation — or a different kind of teacher candidate.

THE NATIONAL TEACHER CORPS AND
TRAINERS OF TEACHER TRAINERS

Both the National Teacher Corps and Trainers of Teacher Trainers were federal initiatives to improve preparation of teachers of disadvantaged students, undertaken on a national scale. They merit close examination for several reasons. First, unlike projects developed by individual schools, Trainers of Teacher Trainers, or TTT as it was generally called, and the Teacher Corps each had dozens of national sites. They faced the organizational challenge of encouraging creative solutions while enforcing standards of achievement, of duplicating successful ideas while protecting against institutionalization of rigid formulas. As I will discuss, the two programs responded to these problems quite differently, and so examination of their respective histories offers important insight about federal attempts to reform education nationally for at-risk students through teacher preparation.

Other characteristics also mark the Teacher Corps for special attention. The program's size and scope were considerable. Between 1965 and 1975, the Teacher Corps prepared about 11,000 people to teach.[61] Programs were located in urban areas, rural Appalachia, Indian reservations, and sites with migrant and Spanish-speaking populations, and were organized with participation by universities and school systems. The Teacher Corps tested, on a national scale, the hypothesis that an internship model of teacher preparation could serve as a mechanism for improving education for the disadvantaged.[62] The initial, "unarticulated expectation that the young might bring freshness and vigor" to public education[63] became an explicit commitment to produce Teacher Corps interns who would be "change agents," introducing curricular innovation to public schools.[64]

Like the Teacher Corps, TTT's importance adheres in the widespread application of its philosophy, in 57 sites in 1970.[65] TTT's philosophy was improvement of education for the disadvantaged through concentrating attention on teacher education personnel themselves, who in turn would improve the quality of teacher preparation programs and the teachers of disadvantaged students. TTT programs retained the traditional base of teacher preparation within college but emphasized institutional change within schools of education to encourage them to share responsibility to "parity" for teacher education with liberal arts faculty, local public schools, and community representatives.[66] While TTT and the Teacher Corps shared a concern about the relevance of teachers' academic preparation, and both experimented with more field-based coursework, the Teacher Corps focused on providing an internship experience that would nurture the individual teacher's ability to prompt change within the public schools. In contrast, TTT attempted to utilize schools of education to alter the relationships among the disparate constituencies of teacher preparation, one of which was the public schools, and in so doing to improve teacher preparation. Thus, analysis of the Teacher Corps and TTT allows comparison of two different approaches to using teacher preparation to improve schooling for the disadvantaged.

The Teacher Corps

The Teacher Corps developed in part from the Cardozo Peace Corps Program, which recruited returning Peace Corps volunteers to staff Cardozo High School in Washington, DC.[67] The Cardozo Project in Urban Teaching, as it was called in the principal's 1964 report, attempted to develop an "intellectual approach to the day-to-day problems of teaching."[68] The project originally had two purposes: to develop effective curricula for school use and to provide teacher training that would "produce teachers who can make the urban classroom a catalyst for those economic, social and intellectual changes which are needed if the public high school is to fulfill its role as a key long-range agent in combatting juvenile delinquency and encouraging youth opportunities."[69]

The traditional teacher preparation program, six months of study followed by six months of teaching, was replaced by an internship model in which participants taught two full classes and attended after-school seminars for coursework leading to certification. Master teachers were hired to teach two classes, supervise the interns, and participate in the after-school seminars taught by professors from nearby colleges and attended by interns and a few regular teachers who were relieved of one of their high school classes. The principal noted that the project engendered some hostility from the school staff, who felt isolated and unutilized. However, their resentment was somewhat ameliorated by the reduction in normal class sizes, which was a result of interns teaching two classes of students who in regular circumstances would have swelled the ranks of the regular faculty's classes. Still, faculty chafed at their exclusion from after-school seminars and the project's failure to assign interns extra duties, like lunchroom patrol, which the rest of the faculty were given. In the second cycle the program addressed these sources of friction: Interns received extracurricular assignments, and regular faculty members were invited to participate in subject matter courses for interns, which were relocated from Howard University to the school.[70]

The overwhelmingly positive evaluation of the initial project prompted its expansion, and recruitment was broadened to include interns who were not returned Peace Corps volunteers. However, a subsequent report showed important conceptual differences between the original Cardozo project and its expanded version, renamed the Urban Teacher Corps.[71] For one, an explicit pedagogical philosophy had been adopted: The program now eschewed the "teacher-dominated, text-oriented, student recitation type" of classroom because it did not meet the needs of inner city youngsters.[72] In addition, the principal's 1964 report stated the program's commitment to produce teachers who would make the classroom a catalyst for broad social and economic change, but it included no negative assessment of the Cardozo faculty or urban teachers generally. The 1968 description of the Urban Teacher Corps outlined a more circumspect goal, attracting and training teachers, but pegged the program's value to the inadequacies of most urban teachers: "ineffective, unconcerned, and ill-prepared persons occupying space in classrooms."[73] In this latter report, the faculty at Cardozo High School, and by implication teachers in most urban high schools, ranged from "a core of dedicated, well-qualified teachers down to the usual number of time-servers."[74]

By 1966 the original program had been replicated in other locations. The programs were funded on two-year cycles, with participation by universities and school systems. Over 750 interns had been graduated and another 900 were completing their final year. Interns enrolled for two years of training and teaching, with steadily increasing teaching responsibility.[75] No entirely "typical" program existed since all were local creations, which changed over their first decade of existence. However, most programs had 33 interns, with the team leaders (the position called "master teacher" in the original project) selected by the principal. The program coordinator was usually a school district employee.[76]

In a special issue of the *Journal of Teacher Education* reporting on the Teacher Corps, two authors identified its goals: to improve educational opportunity for children of the poor; to induct into the teaching establishment college graduates committed to reform; to influence university-based teacher education to become more field-oriented.[77] Senator Gaylord Nelson, who had sponsored the legislation creating the Teacher Corps, described approximately the same objectives: The Teacher Corps was to capture "the idealism and enthusiasm of youth," as the Peace Corps had done, and "to provide quality education for low-income and minority children" by bringing school and university together in teacher education.[78]

These general goals were expressed in Teacher Corps programs in three ways. First, teacher training was considered the vehicle for improving urban education. Second, Teacher Corps interns and graduates were expected as individuals to improve urban education, primarily through curriculum innovations. Finally, much of the coursework for certification was conducted at the school rather than the college, and team leaders at the school sites supervised the practice teaching.

Though the general goals of the Teacher Corps might have been clear, a former director observed that the program never had either a psychology or philosophy of education, aside from training interns as change agents who were "going to straighten things out."[79] Its decentralized organization, as well as sharp disagreements among teacher educators as to appropriate methods of teacher preparation, deterred development of a uniform pedagogical approach. For example, a 1968 evaluation, issued after the first group of interns had been graduated nationally, argued that local programs had to define their criteria for "acceptable teacher preparation in observable or measurable terms" since there were "legitimately conflicting views on the behaviors that constitute competent or effective teaching in different environments or situations."[80] The Teacher Corps' national administration attempted to develop project specifications that would "mesh theory and reality into an integrated, data-dependent, field-based program" in each Teacher Corps project.[81] But this demand for a uniform model of teacher training was resisted by local projects, which argued that standardization led to "oppressive stereotypes" about students and "simple single-minded solutions."[82]

As discussed previously, interns encouraged to be "change agents" and project personnel clashed with regular school staff and "were frequently rejected."[83] The friction between Teacher Corps interns and regular school staff in many Teacher Corps sites mirrored the larger conflict among the Teacher Corps, universities, and school systems. The educational establishment initially expressed reservations about the Teacher Corps bringing interns, who were untrained, into teaching and inviting federal involvement in education, previously the domain of state and local government. In response, Congress amended eligibility requirements and control of intern selection, requiring school systems and cooperating universities to authorize Teacher Corps proposals.[84]

Trainers of Teacher Trainers

Trainers of Teacher Trainers was funded as part of the 1967 Education Professions Development Act. Whether the first "T" in the program title stood for "Trainers" or "Training" was never clear, but the program's focus was understood to be directed to teacher education personnel themselves, and thus indirectly to the teacher candidates they trained. TTT emphasized institutional change within teacher preparation programs, to provide better service to populations least well-served in the past. The concept of developing parity in teacher preparation, which was defined as the participation of schools of education, liberal arts colleges, public schools, and communities in planning and conducting the teacher education program, was one of TTT's central ideas.[85]

By including liberal arts colleges and faculty as partners in reform of teacher preparation, TTT's principle of parity implied that teacher education's flaws were knotted up with defects in higher education as a whole. This theoretical underpinning was articulated in a conference, "The Year of the Liberal Arts," organized by the West Coast and Southwest clusters of TTT to discuss what liberal arts colleges could do to serve the education of teachers and to improve teaching. In all, 43 TTT projects participated, representing four regional groupings.[86] In his introduction to the published version of the conference proceedings, Don Davies argued that "both higher and 'lower' education continue to poison each other's wells; in fact, it turns to be a common well." He maintained that improving elementary and secondary education required reform of higher education, and neither could succeed without genuine participation by the community, which is the interested and main consumer of education.[87]

TTT had a far shorter life-span than the Teacher Corps. Created as part of the 1967 Education Professions Development Act, TTT had its federal funding eliminated by 1973.[88] However, in its brief existence it developed a range of programs so wide that their content and organizational form resist summary. For example, in addition to four different programs at the City University of New York (CUNY), described later, Indiana TTT, based at Indiana University in Bloomington, sponsored an "Urban College Weekend" for school personnel, community members, liberal arts faculty, students, and teacher education faculty. The experience included observation at public schools and immersion in problems and concerns of inner city life, including visits to bars, court, homes of families living on welfare, and a political rally. Indiana TTT also instituted an "Urban Semester Program" for students interested in urban schools, placing students ready to begin their practice teaching in schools for half the semester and in various social service agencies for the other half.[89]

Michigan State University and the Lansing School District attempted to create a new pattern of student teaching in the graduate program as part of their TTT project. The university developed "clinic teams" along subject matter lines (humanities, social science, natural science), with two faculty members from each discipline, a public school teacher, and three experienced teachers serving as fellows. In addition, TTT attempted to stimulate both graduate and undergraduate programs of inner city education that would work with community members to produce materials for teaching.

According to a brochure published by the TTT project of Michigan State University and the Lansing School District, TTT nationally contained 57 sites, which differed in their approach but were all aimed at "in-service development of teacher trainers."[90] Since each project translated the goal of parity into a different programmatic form, no summary presentations of TTT programs is possible, but comparing four co-extant TTT projects of CUNY illuminates the variation in TTT sites, as well as conceptual similarities.

TTT at CUNY, the major trainer of new teachers for New York City, had projects at Hunter, Brooklyn, City, and Richmond Colleges. Each was managed by an advisory board composed of education faculty, liberal arts faculty, public school representatives, students, and community representatives, reflecting the concern with parity. CUNY's TTT stressed making both the faculty and students, undergraduates enrolled in the teacher training program, into teachers and learners, arguing that the real trainers of teachers were people at all levels of education, from elementary pupils to college faculty.[91]

Faculty of Hunter TTT made curriculum planning their focus, involving representatives from the Hunter student body, community, and Harlem public schools. They decided whenever possible to teach liberal arts courses concurrently with related educational methods courses. All TTT students studied Spanish for one year, unless they were already fluent in a language indigenous to an inner city population. The underlying educational philosophy of the project was promoting open classrooms in city schools. Hunter's faculty focused on developing field-based training, with education courses held at the practice-teaching sites. Liberal arts instruction continued at the Hunter campus. Hunter faculty believed that because many of the students in the TTT program were themselves residents of the communities TTT was targeting to serve, including students in decision making addressed the concern for parity. They believed that for organizational reasons, parity was most efficiently translated into "maximum responsiveness to input by TTT students and minimum responsiveness to community input."[92]

Vivian Windley served as TTT project director at City College. The program aimed to improve elementary education in Harlem schools directly, but through this to effect changes in teacher education within the City College program. Parity was attempted by the extensive use of community people as volunteers in open classrooms and the training of para-professionals. Also, liberal arts faculty were recruited as "consultants" from City College to teach public school classes directly and in so doing assist in the inservice aspects of the program. For instance, one sociology professor taught a class to first graders on the functions of families, posing a research question for them about their own family. An evaluation of the lesson noted that the instructor's approach contradicted fundamentals of the open classroom approach, which stressed students' demonstrated readiness for an experience. TTT developed a lab for open education that project participants hoped would be exported, although Windley stressed that not all teachers could or should use open education and that the approach could not succeed without thoroughly prepared teachers, as well as support from the school and community. Student teachers in the TTT project were supervised by "clinical instructors," public school teachers trained by City College.[93]

TTT at Richmond College in Staten Island disintegrated shortly after it began. In his resignation, the program director noted that the project guidelines—to identify groups of change agents among professors of teacher education, professors of liberal arts, public school teachers, parents, community representatives, and college students—had been too vague. Another problem cited in an analysis of the defunct program was hostility between school staff and community members on one side and TTT change agents on the other. Furthermore, although 60% of the Richmond College graduates entered teaching, the liberal arts faculty were skeptical about students' career orientation and the college's career-oriented programs, such as teacher preparation.[94]

Brooklyn College's TTT created a pilot program to transfer teacher training to the public schools in what it termed a "field-centered training model." The program coincided with the major focus of the Brooklyn College teacher education department, which had made the entire senior year of the undergraduate program field-based. While the project cited as a major goal increased participation of public school staff, parents, liberal arts faculty, and community members in teacher education, evaluators reported that it did not meet TTT requirements to have public school personnel, students, and community members educate the teacher trainers. The project's funds were cut and the project director resigned.[95]

Evaluating TTT and the Teacher Corps

Evaluating the success of the Teacher Corps and TTT is problematic because no consensus emerged during the period of this literature review over the fundamental question of whether urban teachers of disadvantaged students required special preparation. Even advocates of specialized preparation of urban teachers differed as to the essential content of such preparation since they disagreed about the reasons for students' academic failure. However, the programs can be judged by their success in accomplishing their respective goals.

Another complication is judging the reliability of the techniques used to assess the programs. Program participants did not always complete questions on evaluation forms if they found them to be irrelevant.[96] However, this limitation should not by itself discredit the evaluations because, especially for TTT, assessments relied heavily on site visits and interviews. For example, an early study of 40 TTT sites had inspection teams of four people, each member a representative of one of the four groups that were to share parity, visit and interview participants.[97] Two prominent participants in TTT and the Teacher Corps have confirmed that my assessment, synthesized from reports, does indeed correspond to their recollection.[98]

Almost all the literature on the change agent strategy of Teacher Corps projects observed that interns made ineffective change agents.[99] Teacher Corps interns trained to be change agents tended to regard "any limitations on their actions to be denials" of their role and "over-react to even reasonable organizational restraints."[100] A summary of data about 10 Teacher Corps projects in 1969–1970 concluded that using interns as change agents created discordance in schools,[101] perhaps because interns were "not infrequently disrespectful of authority, resentful of tradition, impatient with compromise."[102]

A nontechnical summary of data collected on 10 Teacher Corps programs in 1969–1970 observed, "No matter how well-trained the interns or the teachers, it seems unrealistic to hold them responsible for leading school reform while they face the day-to-day, time-consuming tasks and the constraints of their jobs."[103] A director of the National Teacher Corps confirmed this critique when he observed that interns thought they were "going to straighten things out, but it turned out to be a lot tougher than they imagined. Those who had been in the Peace Corps . . . thought it was tougher here by far."[104]

A study that compared graduates of two programs, one of them the Teacher Corps, designed to produce teachers capable of acting as change agents, found that neither change agent group had a greater demand for autonomy than a control group of traditionally trained teachers, but that change agents had a lower sense of power. This result echoes Dunne's objections to M.A.T. change agent programs, which, she said, encouraged an elitist disregard for traditionally trained teachers and areas of shared concern.[105] The Teacher Corps counterposed the "freshness and vigor" that the young interns would bring into schools against the inadequacies of older, experienced staff.[106] In so doing, the Teacher Corps projects did not encourage and probably diminished interns' receptivity to perceiving problems and experiences they shared with veteran teachers. Their high expectations may have fused with a sense of isolation from veteran teachers to create a greater sense of powerlessness.

Gaylord Nelson termed the Teacher Corps "effective and success-ful" in bringing school and university together in teacher education, but the report of the National Advisory Council on Education Professions Development gave a more complicated and critical assessment of the Teacher Corps role. Basing its conclusions on nine studies, the Council noted that institutions of higher education had isolated the Teacher Corps programs and made little change in their teacher training curric-ula; project success depended on the managerial abilities of project participants and their previous organizational relationships; and the more local school districts were involved in training decisions, the less innovation occurred in the classroom. Edelfelt, Corwin, and Hanna also noted tensions between school and university. School districts tended to neglect the Teacher Corps' mission of change to give teachers relief: Teachers wanted interns to be assistants but interns wanted to be change agents. In addition, interns were frequently dissatisfied with the university teaching.[107]

One evaluation concluded that the Teacher Corps succeeded in changing curriculum, but only in classrooms of Teacher Corps graduates, and that student–teacher interaction was not changed. This finding confirmed that teacher education could influence curriculum, which was a primary goal of the Teacher Corps and a valuable one. However, its broader aim of reforming urban schools themselves was unfulfilled. Indeed, the change agent strategy undercut this goal, for in assuming that *individual* teachers could be catalysts for school-wide change, it ignored the *institutional* pressures that caused veteran teachers to perform as they did. Thus, even the young, energetic, idealistic teachers trained by the Teacher Corps were unable to fundamentally alter what their schools taught or how teachers could relate to their students.

The U.S. Office of Education conducted a study of sixth-cycle Teacher Corps graduates, comparing them with other teachers of grades 2 through 6 in the same district. Teacher Corps graduates were superior in developing ethnically relevant curricula, using community resources, and initiating parental contact, but there were no differences in the degree of attention given pupil behavior problems or their affective tone in the classroom. In addition, no differences in students' reading achievement were measured although students of Teacher Corps graduates did score significantly higher on a self-concept scale.[108] Here again, the success of the program was in recruiting and training teachers who could shape instructional content to their students' needs and desires, but individual teachers, no matter how well they accomplished their curricular tasks, could not obviate institutional pressures to deal with students in a custodial fashion. Nor could their curricular improvements boost student scores on standardized reading tests, which was another indication that factors beyond the individual teacher's performance had to be considered in designing teacher education programs that would improve students' achievements.

Ironically, two issues identified as problems for the Teacher Corps were aspects of TTT's raison d'etre. TTT's focus on institutionalization of change addressed the difficulties Teacher Corps projects suffered when they remained isolated within universities, facing sharp resistance to their efforts to reform teacher education curricula.[109] Also, Teacher

Corps project directors learned through painful experience that they had to share power over preparing teachers with school personnel and community groups, and that collaboration had both political and operational aspects that were quite different.[110] For instance, early Teacher Corps projects invited parents and community agencies to vote on the competency of interns, a task that community members asked the professional educators to assume — or to leave community members out of the project entirely. The idea of parity, encouraging participation of all education constituencies in teacher preparation, was a TTT goal from its inception.

The Teacher Corps experience raised "serious questions about whether teacher education can serve as an effective mechanism for educational reform."[111] TTT's experience suggested otherwise. TTT's goal, reform of teacher preparation through the institutional involvement of students, community, school personnel, and liberal arts faculty, was ostensibly less ambitious than the Teacher Corps' objective, sparking systemic change in education for the disadvantaged by attracting and training a different breed of teacher. However, TTT's focus seems to have fostered a capacity for systemic reform that the change agent concept discouraged. TTT's explicit commitment to developing positive, functioning relationships among all teacher education constituencies contradicted the Teacher Corps' conception of the individual teacher's ability to reform schooling.

Sites in both TTT and the Teacher Corps frequently stressed the importance of prospective teachers becoming familiar with the culture and community of their students. Both programs disavowed the idea that the culture of disadvantaged students made them, their families, or their communities incompetent, and both implicitly focused on improving the teacher's ability to link schooling to the child's existence outside the school walls. But these explicit aims of the Teacher Corps were contradicted by its emphasis on the special contribution the new breed of teacher could make, because the focus on the individual teacher's abilities belied the importance of institutional factors.

Although the literature on TTT does not explore this distinction, it appears that TTT applied an *institutional* solution, a change in the power relations among the teacher education constituencies, to what was an *institutional* defect, that is, the failure of urban schools and school systems to adapt to the educational requirements of disadvantaged students. For this reason, when the principle of parity was adhered to, TTT seems to have been successful in developing teacher preparation programs that encouraged innovative teaching techniques that would not otherwise have been accepted by school personnel, parents, and community members.

While there is nothing in the descriptive literature about TTT that makes specific reference to the work of Comer or Riessman, TTT's principle of parity, in effect, expressed the importance of the relationship among education's constituencies. Riessman and Comer identified the relationships among home, family, student, and school as essential to successful education. TTT added higher education and teacher education to the list, supplementing the conceptual purview of Comer's and Riessman's work and reinforcing the idea that substantial improvement in the education of disadvantaged youngsters depended on cooperation, trust, and respect among students, educators, teacher educators, parents, and citizens.

CONCLUSIONS

Several important conclusions can be drawn about the scholarship and programs designed to improve preparation of teachers of disadvantaged students in urban schools in the 1960s.

First, the Teacher Corps experience demonstrated that federal intervention in the preparation of teachers of disadvantaged students could be beneficial, as it was in training teachers to create and select classroom materials that took disadvantaged students' interests and experiences into account. While this important contribution of the Teacher Corps was undercut by its focus on the individual teacher's ability to promote school-wide change, it nonetheless showed that the federal government could play a helpful role in improving the quality of instruction in urban schools by funding programs to improve teachers' skill in developing appropriate materials for their classrooms.

With TTT, the federal government succeeded in creating a program that produced a more effective strategy for introducing change in urban schools. TTT's commitment to parity expressed an educational vision that was clear enough to permit evaluation — and disqualification — of specific sites, yet general enough to encourage diversity and innovation. In contrast, attempting to replicate the success of its original project at Cardozo High School, the Teacher Corps maintained the Cardozo site's organizational components, but lost the sensitivity to local school conditions, which made the initial project successful.

By encouraging local personnel to implement TTT's commitment to parity as they thought best, TTT generated a variety of effective models to improve urban teacher preparation. TTT's formula seems to have effectively addressed the problem of replicating successful projects by replacing the quest for one best system of urban teacher preparation with a quest for multiple solutions. TTT projects failed, as they did at Richmond and Brooklyn Colleges, when local personnel did not understand or were not committed to TTT principles. This raises another organizational problem that TTT did not address, perhaps because of its short-lived existence: How can institutional reform be implemented when local personnel feel no desire to change? Nonetheless, TTT's most important legacy lies not so much in the specific projects that were created under its umbrella but in its commitment and effectiveness in encouraging those ventures.

Second, efforts to generate a definitive list of attributes needed to teach disadvantaged students proved as fruitless as attempts to locate the cause of disadvantagement. The educational *consequences* of disadvantagement were generally agreed upon, but consensus about its causes eluded the educational community. Research considered definitive by advocates of the "culture of poverty" was often summarily rejected by critics of the theory. Further, a research-generated solution to preparation of teachers of disadvantaged students proved illusory. Efforts to solve the problem of disadvantaged children's lack of success in school through research about students' language, behavior, and cognitive abilities, or teachers' values and pedagogical skills, were probably doomed to be rejected by educators whose political thinking caused them to frame the issue differently.

In addition, the political implications of the controversy about the culture of poverty encouraged researchers to examine the problem *either* as one of student deficiency *or* as a limitation of teachers and schools, rather than analyzing the relationship between the components and locating them in a wider context. Because the explanations were presented as mutually exclusive, educators generally failed to recognize the differences among disadvantaged students, as James Comer later noted. The either/or dichotomy of the debate may also explain why educators used "disadvantaged" and "urban" interchangeably to describe the problem: The geographical description was empirically correct and had the virtue of skirting the politically controversial implications of "deprived" and "disadvantaged."

The 1970s: Competency-Based and Multicultural Teacher Education

Important changes in the nation's political climate altered the terms of debate from the late 1960s through the early 1980s about educating "disadvantaged" students in urban schools. However, debate in the education community remained polarized over the source of academic failure. In this second period, new strategies to improve education for disadvantaged students in urban schools emerged, most important, competency-based teacher education, multicultural education, and the effective schools movement. However, they embodied the earlier polarization between authors who located responsibility for the academic failure of disadvantaged students in students' cognitive or social inadequacies and others who faulted teachers' skills and attitudes for lack of student achievement. One striking difference in this next phase of scholarship was the evaporation of material advocating that urban teachers, either as change agents or unionists, transform school structures that blocked student achievement. In fact, only the effective schools proponents discussed how characteristics of urban school systems affected student performance.

MULTICULTURAL EDUCATION

Attempts by civil rights activists to remedy educational inequalities for black students sparked similar efforts by other ethnic groups, as well as advocates of expanded opportunities for women and the physically handicapped.[1] By 1970 writers had begun to describe American schools' "rich diversity" of students: Puerto Rican students in eastern cities; Chinese, Japanese, and Pacific Islands immigrants in the western states; Mexican Americans in the midwest and southwest; Cubans in Florida; and black and native Americans throughout the country. In addition, immigrants concentrated in a particular metropolitan area, for instance, the Asian Indians in New York City, demanded recognition of their needs.[2]

This growing concern that nonwhite, nonnative speakers of English were being educationally shortchanged enlarged the category of disadvantaged students. A new strategy, multicultural education, developed, reflecting this awareness. The *Thesaurus of* ERIC *Descriptors* introduced the term *multicultural education* in 1979, defining it as "education involving two or more ethnic groups and designed to help participants clarify their own ethnic identity and appreciate that of others, reduce prejudice and stereotyping, and promote cultural pluralism and equal participation."[3]

Advocates of multicultural education focused on the need to change teachers' "expectations, attitudes and strategies," which, they argued, caused student failure because an

> unconscious reflex rooted in the teacher's own middle class background combined with training which consciously or unconsciously may not recognize the possibility of alternative cultural styles and cognitive modes. This combination results in a middle American ethnocentricism [sic] which is destructive to minority students, students from poor families, and any other student who deviates from the mythical norm espoused in teacher training institutions.[4]

Writers who placed responsibility for students' academic failure on "culturally deficient educators" advocated changes in teacher education to instruct all prospective teachers, but most especially those who taught students from racial and language minorities, that cultural diversity was a positive value. In this perspective, teachers above all needed skills that were consonant with students' ethnic, cultural, and linguistic background.[5]

The introduction of multicultural education paralleled substitution of the generic term "disadvantaged" for the more controversial label "culturally deprived." A search of ERIC shows 444 entries using *culturally disadvantaged* as a key term from 1966 to 1975 but only 51 from 1976 to 1982. By 1980, the more general word *disadvantaged* had supplanted use of *socially* and *culturally disadvantaged* in the *Thesaurus of* ERIC *Descriptors*."[6] Frank Riessman altered his book title from *The Culturally Deprived Child* to *The Inner City Child* because the title was "entirely inappropriate." Riessman noted that "new material and thinking" since its publication in 1962 had compelled him to revise its entire contents.[7]

The popularity of multicultural education was fed by two other political changes, both alluded to in the literature but frequently ignored in scholarly debate. First, an economic recession, exacerbated by taxpayer revolts, led to drastic reductions in state and federal expenditures for education and to the nation's cities.[8] Large city school systems, like the cities they served, were faced with severe fiscal problems.[9] Expenditures per pupil for schools in central cities were consistently below those for schools outside the central city, although the educational needs of inner city students were demonstrably greater. Correcting this "inadequacy, inequity, and disparity" in school funding was the prerequisite for improving urban schools, but it was a political task confounded by another critical development, an acknowledged failure to racially integrate urban schools.[10] While writers disputed the reasons urban schools became more racially segregated, the reality was incontrovertible. By the early 1970s, large city schools mostly served a population of racial and ethnic minority children, especially in the older neighborhoods, called the inner or central city.[11]

MULTICULTURAL EDUCATION AND COMMUNITY CONTROL OF SCHOOLS

The defeat of efforts to integrate urban schools led to demands for the "transfer of decision-making powers" to the residents of racially segregated schools.[12] Though not a unanimously accepted strategy, this idea, which became known as "community control," had a significant following.[13] Like the advocates of multicultural education, writers who defended community control did so with arguments about the ways in which teachers' skills and attitudes caused student failure. One author explained that teachers needed "competency skills" for selecting materials for the black experiences, but the most crucial element in their success was an understanding of "personal bias and prejudices that might be injected into teaching."[14] Historians argued about whether this development represented a unique shift toward ethnocentrism in American politics, as Diane Ravitch contended, or a challenge to the dominant ethnocentrism of those "behavioral and cultural models . . . exhibited by the American descendants of Northern Europeans," as Edgar Epps maintained.[15]

Whether because of cuts in funding for research or diminished interest in the subject, urban schools receded from the educational spotlight in this period. In Phi Delta Kappa's examination of the major issues confronting the teaching profession in the 1970s the editor noted that "to many critics, the problems of the inner-city school seem insoluble."[16] Perhaps the intractability of urban school problems discouraged the authors in the collection, for none discussed problems of teaching disadvantaged students or the conditions in city schools, arguably two of the profession's most important problems.

"HEREDITARIANS" AND "ENVIRONMENTALISTS"

In reviewing pertinent research from 1960 to 1980 on educating inner city children, Allan C. Ornstein devised two categories, "environmentalists" and "hereditarians." He argued that environmentalists Benjamin Bloom, J. McVicker Hunt, and Martin Deutsch used social and economic factors, such as family setting, cognitive styles, or family income, to explain students' lack of achievement. On the other side were hereditarians, such as Arthur Jensen, William Shockley, and Richard Herrnstein, who attributed academic failure to inherited deficiencies.[17]

Although Ornstein adopted the geographic label "inner city" to describe poor students, especially those who were black, his study reflected the same underpinning as earlier work on cultural deprivation. The sources of disadvantagement had changed to heredity and environment, but the underlying theory remained: School failure was caused by student characteristics. The two causes, heredity and environment, were not subject to student or parent control, but they produced the symptoms that resulted in educational failure. However, Ornstein's research synthesis omitted reference to the other body of literature, which blamed the school environment or teacher characteristics for student failure, ignoring material on multicultural education, community control, or the characteristics of effective schools.

Debate over the hereditarian research focused on its basic premise rather than on implementation of the ideas. By suggesting that student failure was genetically driven, the hereditarians in effect undercut arguments about the need for educational change, since biology, not schooling, caused academic success. On the other hand, for the environmentalists whose work Ornstein described, boosting the academic achievement of disadvantaged students was primarily a matter of increasing government spending to assist minority children to "overcome educational disadvantages of home and environment."[18]

Another group of writers whom Ornstein ignored could also be considered environmentalists, since they argued that school reform could not substantially reduce "the extent of cognitive inequality, as measured by tests of verbal fluency, reading comprehension, or mathematical skill. Neither school resources nor segregation has any appreciable effect on either test scores or educational achievement," they maintained.[19] These environmentalists contended that schooling could not reduce inequality; that would require economic, not educational, reforms, for instance, use of income subsidies. Like the hereditarians, they concluded that school reform would do little to correct social inequality. Although they themselves did not identify their perspective as

a "schools don't make a difference" argument, their research and point
of view were commonly associated with this viewpoint.[20]

> Our research suggests, however, that the character of a school's output
> depends largely on a single input, namely the characteristics of the
> entering children. Everything else—the school budget, its policies,
> the characteristics of the teachers—is either secondary or completely
> irrelevant.[21]

Frank Riessman was one of the few writers who attempted to move
beyond the polarization between environmentalists and hereditarians.
He contended that the debate about the role of heredity and environment in relation to academic achievement was "abstract and absurd"
since "hereditary factors can only occur to the extent the environment
brings them out."[22] He argued that research such as the studies Jencks
used, which revealed no widespread benefits from the educational programs initiated in the 1960s, was misleading because its broad scope
did not reflect the success of individual projects. Addressing arguments
about schooling's inability to correct inequality, Riessman explained
that programs had failed to significantly improve the learning of inner
city children because teachers used a compensatory model to try to
make the inner city child resemble a middle class child and, further,
did not know how to develop students' higher level skills. But he also
argued that structural change in urban school systems and the management of individual schools were essential to improve academic achievement of inner city children. Exclusive attention to "training and scape-
goating teachers"[23] had obfuscated the importance of "change of the
[school] organization and the system," he wrote.[24] However, Riessman
also warned that improving environmental conditions, most important,
creating full employment, was the single most critical measure the government could take to bolster educational achievement among inner
city children.

OCEAN HILL–BROWNSVILLE

The dispute about the causes of and solutions to minority children's
academic failure occurred in its most politically charged form in 1968
and 1969, when leaders of the United Federation of Teachers (UFT),
the New York City teachers' union with a mostly white membership,
confronted the mainly black and Puerto Rican advocates of a plan
to decentralize administrative control of the city schools. The conflict

resulted in a long, bitter strike named after the Brooklyn neighborhoods of Ocean Hill and Brownsville where the dispute erupted. Debate about the strike's purposes and effects stretched far beyond New York City's borders and echoed for years thereafter.[25] Ocean Hill–Brownsville became a synonym and symbol for the collapse of hope that teachers, parents, and community members could work together.[26] However, the conflict was rarely analyzed in the context of both diminished funding for school improvement and the defeat of school integration efforts, although both were matters of record.[27]

Shortly before the strike began, the UFT attempted to use its position in contract negotiations to win funding for its More Effective Schools (MES) program, designed to improve target schools serving poor, minority students. The program called for decreasing class size dramatically; grouping students heterogeneously; providing additional supplies, materials, and counselors; and involving parents and community members in school management. In a development that was soon replicated on a national scale, the board of education reduced funding for the program because, officials argued, the board could no longer rely on federal spending for school programs. Also, some community representatives questioned whether test scores of students in the pilot program had risen enough to justify the massive expenditures.[28] Furthermore, the premise of the program was in itself objectionable to some educators, who saw MES removing responsibility for students' failure from the school system and placing it on the family and community. MES was faulted for tying academic achievement to the success of efforts to "approximate the environmental conditions of suburban schools in inner city schools," an approach that its critics complained condemned a whole way of life as inadequate.[29]

Linking the problem of reduced federal school aid to the failure of school integration, David Cohen predicted the collision between the community and teachers' union a year before the strike began. He argued that community control was a strategy designed to substitute for racial integration, an understandable but harmful response to the civil rights movement's failure to integrate the city schools. Cohen maintained that the community control strategy ignored the dire need for massive resource reallocation and, in fact, dampened prospects for mounting a popular challenge to the reductions in federal aid.[30]

The UFT and its MES strategy also accepted, implicitly, segregated schooling, and in so doing ignored the barriers to learning inherent in schooling segregated by race and class, Cohen argued. Yet, even vast amounts of money poured into ghetto schools would scarcely begin to compensate for their racial and social isolation. Thus, neither MES nor community control could succeed in significantly altering conditions in poor city schools, he argued, because in bowing to segregated schooling, each sacrificed the political mainspring of a successful campaign to revise the nation's social and political priorities and win the new funds needed to improve urban education.[31]

COMPETENCY-BASED TEACHER EDUCATION

The bitter controversy about the poor academic achievement of minority students combined with funding cuts for schools to swell support for a new strategy to improve teacher preparation for urban schools: competency-based teacher education. Beginning in the early 1970s, competency-based or performance-based teacher education (CBTE and PBTE) dominated discourse about teacher education.[32] Both CBTE and PBTE were introduced in the *Thesaurus of ERIC Descriptors* in 1972, with CBTE supplanting PBTE in March 1980.[33] From 1966 to 1975, a period of nine years, ERIC recorded 478 articles and papers using "CBTE" as a major descriptor; in the six years 1976 to 1982 the number jumped to 1,555, about the same number who were using "compensatory education" (1,593) and "multicultural education" (1,202) as major descriptors. One author noted, "Rarely, if ever, has any movement swept through teacher education so rapidly or captured the attention of so many in so short a time as has the competency-based movement."[34] A 1981 report on CBTE's acceptance in institutions affiliated with the American Association of Colleges for Teacher Education (AACTE) noted that 59% of the respondents (79% of AACTE's 787 members) confirmed that they were operating programs "for the most part" based on CBTE.[35]

Components of CBTE programs varied widely, but one description, identified as the "best-known" definition, outlined the following essential characteristics: Students' progress depended on their ability to perform satisfactorily discrete teaching tasks or competencies. The competencies were to be based on actual teaching conditions, stated to teacher-candidates in advance so they would know what they were supposed to accomplish, and subjected to public scrutiny. The teacher preparation program had to assist the student in acquiring these competencies, usually in an individualized format, known as an "instructional module."[36]

Critics of CBTE objected to its underlying premise that teaching could be divided into discrete skills, its "claim to scientific stature," and the attempt to standardize teaching through formal performance criteria, which they argued suited schooling's bureaucratic, not peda-gogical, needs.[37] "The idea that there are specific classroom situations to be handled by special skills learned in specific modules of teacher training is a bureaucratic dream quite divorced from the realities of the modern classroom," one educator fumed.[38] Another author argued that CBTE's "allegedly systematic nature" was contradicted by its reliance on primarily prescriptive teaching and learning theories.[39] Furthermore, CBTE overlooked the influence of the teacher's values and attitudes, since, by definition, only what could be assessed objectively could be included. CBTE's claim to individualize teacher preparation, drawing the teacher-candidate into his or her own training, was bogus because at the onset of any module, the teacher-in-training would not know that skills were needed. Finally, CBTE failed to draw distinctions among the values of the various competencies.[40]

To a great extent, CBTE was driven by mandates from state legisla-tures, which used their authority over teacher licensing and certifica-tion to introduce CBTE into teacher preparation. A survey of state edu-cation departments conducted in 1972 revealed just how widespread were interest in and support for adoption of CBTE: Nine states were evaluating the idea, six were launching evaluations, thirteen were working for future implementation, seven states were watching for de-velopments in other states, and seven had changed licensing provisions to allow for competency-based certification. Only two states stated they had no interest in CBTE.[41]

If the extent to which CBTE was actually adopted by programs preparing urban teachers remains in doubt, what is indisputable is its political draw. What explains this political magnetism? Two early proponents of CBTE attributed its appeal to the convergence of four changes in education: the heightened awareness of subcultures and their problems in society; schools' increasing inability to perform tradi-tional functions; research developments that provided new information into instructional methodology; and application of new technologies and management systems, as well as concern about the impact of tech-nological change.[42]

The perception that schools were failing to educate students was translated into a concern that schools and teachers should be made accountable for students' academic failures. The notion of accountabil-ity was borrowed from models of product delivery systems used in business. In schooling, the product, or "output," was the achievement level of the learner; the accountable parties were those responsible for some part of the educational process, or the "input" to the product delivery system.[43] The difficulty in applying this model to schooling, as even enthusiastic proponents of CBTE admitted, was that there was no irrefutable evidence that certain inputs were more successful than others. One author noted that the attributes of successful inner city teachers could not be deduced from research because there was so little available. Instead, she argued, educators must rely on "intuition, observation, and experience."[44] Similarly, an early evaluation of the Teacher Corps recommended that local programs "define their criteria of acceptable teacher preparation in observable or measurable terms" because there are "legitimately conflicting views on the behaviors that constitute competent or effective teaching in different environments or situations."[45]

CBTE, as both its supporters and critics understood, implicitly promised to de-politicize the debate over the skills and attitudes teachers needed by analyzing teaching behavior in terms of competencies that could be evaluated objectively. This made CBTE's political appeal almost ineluctable, since it seemed to break the impassioned stand-off between reformers who blamed teachers for minority student failure and those who found student characteristics at fault for poor academic achievement. However, CBTE was not neutral in this debate; its popularity marked the ideological ascendancy of the perspective that located student failure in teacher characteristics. Its exclusive focus on improving education through teachers' acquisition of skills and attitudes negated the possibility that material conditions, like full employment and school management, as Frank Riessman argued, or school characteristics, as Ron Edmonds contended, shaped student performance.

CBTE's gathering strength mirrored the waning influence of educators who advocated compensatory programs, as well as urban teachers and their unions. By the mid-1970s, teacher organizations had been seriously weakened by the fiscal problems that buffeted school districts, most especially urban systems, as well as by demographic changes that reduced the size of the school population. For example, almost one-quarter of all the pedagogical employees in the New York City schools were laid off during the city's budget crisis in 1974–1975; over 15,000 teachers and counselors lost their jobs.[46]

The organizational rivalry between the National Education Association (NEA) and the American Federation of Teachers (AFT) encouraged each to present membership figures in the most advantageous way, so it is difficult to ascertain the exact number of teachers who lost their jobs. Since the AFT represented teachers in the largest urban systems, however, its membership figures were especially revealing. AFT president Albert Shanker's 1976–1977 report to the union claimed a net loss of 30,000 members. He noted that "we did not bring enough members into the AFT to offset the devastating effects of reductions in force due to budget crises and the decreasing numbers of students." He compared the AFT's membership decline to the NEA's "proportionately larger loss of 100,000 or 200,000 or 300,000 members," depending on which of the NEA's figures "you choose to believe."[47]

The loudest opposition to CBTE came from teacher organizations, especially the AFT. The Committee on Performance-Based Teacher Education of the American Association of Colleges for Teacher Education agreed that CBTE had "positive potential" and was "one of the possible teacher education types that deserves development," but warned that it could easily lend itself to "programs based only on teaching the simplest mechanical behaviors and those dealing solely with cognitive behavior at that."[48]

In contrast, Eugenia Kemble, writing for the AFT, found nothing to recommend CBTE. She charged that the schools of education had greeted state mandates for CBTE warmly because of the demographic crunch diminishing the supply of new teachers and the need for teacher preparation. CBTE accommodated a shift to inservice education for teachers already employed, protecting positions and budgets for teacher training institutions. School boards liked CBTE because it provided a rationale and method to replace old (highly paid) teachers with new (lower paid) ones. Like many other authors, Kemble attributed CBTE's popularity to the political climate, but she argued that CBTE's appeal relied on the convergence of pressure to cut government expenditures with the idea that public schools were failing. Kemble maintained that dissatisfaction with the schools was unfounded: "Together the school critics and moneyed urban liberals were pushing the view that the schools were no good and that what needed to be changed was the people in them and the way they are controlled."[49]

Kemble's other major criticism of CBTE was voiced by other educators and organizations, but her objections were stated in the harshest language, which was perhaps a reflection of the fear that Ornstein and Talmage noted some white urban teachers felt. Performance objectives were "ludicrous," Kemble wrote, and they made a "mockery of the profession."[50] Assessment in CBTE was "shallow and simplistic," and the "vindictive political implications" for teachers would "be fought," she warned.[51]

One significant aspect of Kemble's critique that was not remarked upon was its reversal of the union's earlier insistence that school reform was its ultimate goal. Ten years before, the AFT had been among the school critics demanding a change in the way schools were controlled, as demonstrated by provisions in MES that encouraged parent and teacher involvement in decision making. In 1975, the chair of the AFT Task Force on Educational Issues downplayed the urgency of school reform.

Curiously, few authors discussed the connections between CBTE's rising star, the economic recession, and the diminished concern about structural reform of urban school systems. For example, while Kemble saw that CBTE's appeal was in part financial, a response to cutbacks in government funding, she ignored the impact of reduced federal funding for programs to reform urban schools. Allan Ornstein and Harriet Talmage described the ideological character of the debate over accountability and the growing fear of many white teachers and administrators in big cities that these programs would "be used as a weapon against them — and not for educational purposes."[52] But they attributed the implementation of CBTE and accountability programs to "liberal bandwagon wisdom and black militant ideology," neglecting the leading role the federal government had played in encouraging CBTE, through the U.S. Office of Education's model projects and the Teacher Corps.[53]

Similarly, Gaylord Nelson explained that the "overall surplus of teachers" in the early 1970s made the Teacher Corps shift its focus from preparing new teachers to improving the quality of teachers already serving in schools in low-income areas. Another report on the Teacher Corps noted that its 1970–1972 guidelines were changed to reflect the movement toward competency-based programs, as a result of the findings of the federal Model Elementary Teacher Education Program. Neither report analyzed the relationship between CBTE and teacher employment patterns, nor their link to the economic recession.[54]

CBTE AND MULTICULTURAL EDUCATION

CBTE became especially attractive as a strategy for improving urban schools, perhaps because both financial strains and racial tensions were most severe in large school districts and, when joined to multicultural education, CBTE addressed both problems, as I will explain. By 1973, the American Association of State Colleges and Universities, whose members historically educated half of the country's teachers, had instituted "an experiment in planned change" to encourage competency-based urban teacher education by funding planning grants.[55]

Because CBTE attempted to standardize and evaluate teaching skills, and multicultural education focused on changing teachers' attitudes, the two strategies seemed to be pedagogically and politically counterposed. But they shared two assumptions that made them natural partners. First they were both predicated on the belief that improving education for urban students, now mainly from minority groups, depended on correcting teacher deficiencies. Also, both strategies relied on identifying discrete abilities teachers needed for success. A union of the two strategies soon developed: multicultural CBTE. As one advocate of multicultural education wrote in endorsing its marriage to CBTE, "If there is a recognized need for restructuring our educational system, CBTE can be the vehicle" because it "recognizes individual differences as positive" and demands a wide range of sources for determining competencies, "sources not heeded in the past." Finally it provided accountability through the "externalization of assumptions under which desired outcomes" were determined, that is, by baring the cultural biases which blocked success for minority students.[56]

A report issued jointly by two committees of AACTE, one on multicultural education, the other on CBTE, outlined their agreements. Teachers "need certain unique competencies in order to teach in culturally diverse situations," the editor noted.[57] Another writer explained that "for most Blacks, bad teaching . . . is most often less a matter of a teacher's deficit in commonly practiced teaching skills than a matter of the reflection of a teacher's fundamentally negative feelings or expectations for Black children."[58] Multicultural CBTE focused on the attitudes teachers needed, as opposed to cognitive skills, since the teacher's primary role was defined as the "facilitator of the acquisition of value systems consonant with a student's ethnic, cultural and linguistic background."[59] However, CBTE and multicultural education could be wedded only in a theoretical framework that ignored school structure: Accommodating students' cultural needs would require greater curricular flexibility, but the more schools diversified their offerings and allowed teachers freedom to adapt to students' needs, the more difficult it would be to evaluate teacher or student performances according to uniform standards, the *sine qua non* of CBTE.[60] Since urban school structures were discussed so little in this period, this contradiction went virtually unnoticed.

RESEARCH AND TEACHER EDUCATION

The hope of refining teaching's knowledge base to resolve political challenges to the profession's authority was certainly not new.[61] However, it blossomed with CBTE as teachers, teacher educators, and schools felt themselves under attack. Earlier, an editorial in *The Urban Review* had predicted just this development: As the urban educator's personal authority was diminished because of racial conflict, and as the authority bestowed by the educational system itself was challenged, his or her reliance on specialized knowledge, "technocratic" skill, would increase.[62]

"Can science contribute to the art of teaching?" N. L. Gage asked in 1972. He answered that it would be

> nice if the answer could be a resounding "Yes" based on a long parade of conclusive evidence and examples of richly useful findings. Unfortunately . . . the question must receive a rather more complex response.[63]

Indeed, one of the primary arguments against CBTE was that it relied on an inadequate knowledge base, or rather one that could be used to defend contradictory propositions about teacher performance. Three researchers concluded that assessment of teacher effectiveness at the level of pupil achievement was not possible because, according to available research, more than 90% of the variance in student test scores was attributable to unknown influences, that is, factors other than teacher effectiveness. Their report argued that teacher educators "need to know many more things about the behavior of a teacher and the characteristics of pupils in order to identify the special teacher behaviors which are effective for particular pupils."[64] This analysis is confirmed by examining three contradictory interpretations of a key study by Rosenshine and Furst on improving teacher performance. Some authors used it to buttress their commitment to CBTE, another educator employed it to confirm his opposition to CBTE, and yet a third group found that the study supported their compromise about how and when CBTE would be appropriate.[65]

Furthermore, Gage, himself a leading researcher, contended that the value of scientific knowledge about what constituted successful teacher behavior depended on the inference that the behavior was related to something desirable.[66] However, deciding what expectations teachers could or should have of students was precisely the political controversy that CBTE, and especially multicultural CBTE, was supposed to resolve. The inherent limitation of attempting to use research to resolve what was a political dilemma was illustrated when the Educational Testing Service worked out a method of evaluating student progress with the UFT and the New York City Board of Education in 1972. The program faltered when the parties could not agree on what aspects of student performance to measure or on how to correlate teacher rewards with student achievement.[67]

Indeed, even if research could refine understanding of how students learned what teachers taught, one major obstacle remained in improving academic achievement of "cuturally different" students: Conditions in urban schools, where they were concentrated, made application of the knowledge problematic at best. A well-known researcher who returned to teach full-time in an urban elementary school for a year, determined to put into practice some of the ideas she had been teaching and writing about, described how "objective problems," like overcrowding and class size, undermined her efforts.[68] Yet the literature failed to connect teacher behavior, student performance, and school characteristics.

One notable exception to this was Mary Haywood Metz's study of two junior high schools in a small metropolitan system recently desegregated. The author explored how the culture of the faculty, the history of the school, the size and design of the school building, and the principal's philosophy and leadership style all influenced the ways that students, parents, and teachers responded to desegregation. Metz's research assumed that "studies of the effectiveness of various teaching styles can only be meaningful when they specify in subtle detail the character of the children taught and the context of the school and school district."[69] By introducing the contextual influences on teacher performance, Metz implicitly dismissed CBTE's claim to have identified and standardized the competencies teachers needed. She argued that the processes through which students learned were "poorly understood" and educators lacked "any universally effective means" or any "trustworthy way of measuring the success or failure of whatever methods they finally apply."[70]

It is interesting to note that Metz's research was conducted in a community and school system that voluntarily committed themselves to racially integrate their public schools. As she noted, this made the community a political exception, but her study may illustrate again how the failure of efforts to desegregate urban school systems contributed to the diminution of interest in the institutional characteristics of urban schools. Undergirding CBTE and multicultural education was an acquiescence to political developments that made structural transformation of urban schools seem impossible. Little research investigated how the characteristics of urban schools influenced teacher performance, and discussion about characteristics of urban schools and school systems remained peripheral to the dominant concerns about CBTE and multicultural education.[71]

EFFECTIVE SCHOOLS

The most important challenge to scholarly preoccupation with teacher and student characteristics was the effective schools strategy (a different phenomenon from the MES program the UFT advocated in 1966). Popularized by Ronald Edmonds, at one time director of the Center for Urban Studies at Harvard Graduate School of Education, the effective schools strategy was a response to the "schools-don't-matter" arguments of Jencks and Coleman.[72] Its purpose was to demonstrate that there were schools for poor, minority children that succeeded in boosting academic achievement and then identify the common characteristics of these schools in order to replicate their success.

Underlying the effective schools strategy was the assumption that urban school districts, impoverished and torn by racial strife, required external change agents to spark change. Unlike the change agent strategies of the 1960s, which gave teachers responsibility for crystallizing structural reform of schools, Edmonds saw teachers' primary role as having a "subservient and receptive frame of mind" to deliver the services that communities desired.[73] Teachers were "decent men and women who work hard and conscientiously strive to benefit the needful portions of our population."[74] However, their importance in school improvement was limited to understanding that their clients were also their constituents, that is, that their job was to provide the service that parents and community members requested. Although Edmonds argued that teachers were "internal advocates for reform," their responsibilities were completely reactive and resulted from their access to insider knowledge. Edmonds emphasized the importance of dialogue between parents and teachers, but his model of conversation consisted of parents telling teachers what services were desired and teachers providing information about how resources could best be used. The one attitude that Edmonds required of teachers was rejection of the "cultural autocracy" that labeled children of color deficient. Hence, one of the characteristics of an effective school was that teachers showed high expectations for all students.[75]

The only other trait of an effective school that related to teacher performance was the use of standardized achievement tests to monitor student performance.[76] This characteristic was tied to Edmonds's theory that goals for school improvement in "abstract and grandiloquent" terms were "tactically disastrous."[77] In arguing for measuring schools, teachers, and students' performance with minimal standards that allowed external monitoring, Edmonds addressed a political change, the reduced interest — or hope — in urban school improvement. Though urban schools could not satisfy a "grand" goal, like delivering a quality education to all black children, at least they could succeed with the minimal tasks of teaching the literacy and numeracy skills measured on achievement tests. This accomplishment could "persuade poorly served communities that they need not despair of improvement in the quality of social service now available to them" and presumably prompt even greater reform.[78] In addition, he implicitly acknowledged the legacy of Ocean Hill–Brownsville, explaining that his "language of minimums" could "neutralize a hostile social service setting"[79] to allow the teacher to determine "whether or not progress is being made."[80] Though Edmonds acknowledged that the tests did not "adequately measure the appropriate ends of education," he argued that they were "the most realistic, accurate, and equitable basis for portraying individual pupil progress."[81] Edmonds applied his ideas in New York City, where he designed a School Improvement Plan that used his "language of minimums." He argued that a uniform district-wide curriculum and uniform standards were essential for school improvement because they held schools to an observable, externally verifiable standard of achievement, in the same way that the tests monitored student progress. Within this context of a standardized curriculum, teachers would be given "the widest possible latitude in deciding textual materials, classroom organization, instructional strategy."[82] Furthermore, the teacher's diminished discretion in deciding what to teach paralleled the principal's enhanced importance, since another characteristic of an effective school was that the principal identified and diagnosed institutional problems.[83] Thus, the effective schools strategy that Edmonds advocated contained circumscribed pedagogical and political roles for teachers. Their responsibilities within the classroom were limited since curricula and standards were uniform, established by a central authority; their role in deciding school policies contracted as the principal's importance expanded. Since teachers' skills and attitudes were peripheral to improving schools and student achievement, so was teacher education. The one attitude Edmonds required of urban teachers, their rejection of "cultural autocracy," was already addressed in multicultural education. Thus, the effective schools model contained little to inspire new strategies for preparing urban teachers.[84]

CONCLUSIONS

Scholarship in the 1970s reflected reduced concerns and demands about improving the achievement of disadvantaged students in urban schools. The two shifts in terminology used to describe students previously identified as deprived or disadvantaged mirrored the increasing racial and social isolation of poor, minority students and reductions in government funding for urban schools. Describing urban students as culturally diverse was accurate in one sense, an acknowledgment of the many different racial and immigrant communities that sought political recognition of their presence in metropolitan areas. But in another sense, the new description failed to address a second, less hopeful political change: Advocates of racial integration had failed in their efforts to make urban schools racially and socially balanced. Similarly, adoption of the term *inner city* signaled the effort to move beyond the polarization of educators about the causes of low academic achievement of poor, minority children who were concentrated in urban school systems. The term *inner city*, introduced in the *Thesaurus of ERIC Descriptors* in 1966 to mean the "central section of a city which is usually older and more densely populated," may have connoted poverty and decay to the knowledgeable reader, but it did not denote these conditions as the related terms *ghettos* and *slums* had. Yet, inner city schools were indeed more impoverished and isolated than they had been 10 years earlier when writers referred to slum schools.

What explains these linguistic denials of social conditions? Because this question wasn't posed, it wasn't answered in the literature. However, it seems to me that there are three explanations. First, chastened by criticism of their work about cultural deprivation, many educators were eager to avoid characterizing anything about poor, minority students as a deficit, even poverty. Whether their thinking had been changed by the debate over cultural deprivation or they simply wished to avoid conflict is probably impossible to ascertain, but it is significant that the change in nomenclature did not erase the political disagreement. As the controversy over the research of the hereditarians shows, the disagreement persisted.

Second, these semantic sleights of hand allowed educators to retain their commitment to improve urban schools in the face of a political climate that made the task seem, to many, impossible.

Finally, the change in language paralleled the ascendancy of strategies that assumed that pupil learning was a function only of teachers' skills and attitudes, most notably, CBTE. It stands to reason that CBTE had only a limited practical effect on urban teacher preparation because urban school districts were laying off, not hiring, teachers, and schools of education accommodated to the new job market (for teachers and teacher educators) by redirecting their attention to inservice education. However, CBTE had a profound influence on the way educators discussed and conceptualized teaching. The terms *performance* and *competencies* gained acceptance as the lingua franca for evaluating a teacher's work.

The ostensibly value-free terminology for identifying acceptable teaching behavior, which was part of CBTE's ineluctable appeal, in fact represented a distinct set of values. CBTE's input/output model defined "input" as *teacher* input, with schooling's social context, including funding levels and social isolation of minority students, eliminated from the equation. Unlike educators who argued that conditions in urban schools had to change for teaching to improve, or that social conditions, like high levels of unemployment, depressed student achievement, CBTE's proponents implied that teaching behavior was unrelated to these external factors. CBTE presumed that technical expertise was the key to improved teaching and learning, in sharp distinction to the implicit goals of the Teacher Corps and TTT, which made curricular reform and parity the pivotal methods of improving education for urban youngsters.

However, it is important to understand that CBTE's ascendancy was encouraged by developments in both TTT and the Teacher Corps. Neither program had *explicitly* addressed the need for programs preparing urban teachers of disadvantaged students to take into account the political and social context of the schools in which their graduates would teach. Certainly, TTT's goal of parity — developing a shared vision of schooling's means and ends — implied that the context of teaching and learning was more critical than acquisition of discrete skills or techniques. However, the absence of any articulated perspective about the interrelationship among teaching, learning, school conditions, and social influences on school performance, contributed to the legitimacy of CBTE's decontextualized approach to teacher preparation. Like TTT, the Teacher Corps also contributed to CBTE's ascendancy. Although it placed teachers at the center of curricular reform and identified curricular reform, in turn, as a pivotal method of improving education for urban students, the Teacher Corps' failure to address the *institutional* role that teachers had to assume in this process, and its dedication to the idea of the individual teacher's abilities, allowed CBTE to reduce curricular change to a formulaic process that ignored the school conditions that the Teacher Corps was committed to altering.

During this period, advocates of multicultural education and effective schools criticized the federal government's use of compensatory programs that relied on a deficit model to explain and reverse the academic failure of poor, minority children. Ironically, few noted the leading role the Office of Education took in encouraging CBTE, a reform that ignored all the material barriers to improving urban schools, and in so doing dismissed the problems in theory while aggravating them in practice. Teacher unionists, the constituency that argued most consistently about the need to alter school conditions, had lost much of its political influence. The union's argument that the "teacher surplus" was driven by budgetary rather than educational needs failed to gain widespread public support. The other voices for reform, those proposing CBTE, multicultural education, and effective schools to improve the education of urban students, made no reference to the material conditions in urban schools that sabotaged efforts to improve instruction.

Even more than before, discourse was fragmented, divided between educators who blamed student failure on school conditions and those who described student or teacher failings. Mirroring the neglect and isolation of the urban schools themselves, debate about preparing teachers of poor, minority students in urban schools unraveled until it was little more than a series of monologues, with proponents of CBTE, effective schools, multicultural education, and teacher unionism seldom addressing shared concerns — or each other.

The 1980s: Excellence and Equity

Beginning in 1983, with publication of *A Nation at Risk*, the quality of the nation's schools, students, and teachers became an important policy issue for federal and state government. A report issued by prominent business and government leaders warned that the educational system was eroded by a "rising tide of mediocrity" that imperiled the nation's ability to compete economically.[1] While educators debated the assumptions and conclusions of the report, they agreed that it sparked a "tidal wave of reports that sought to reform America's schools."[2] In his introduction to a symposium published by the *Harvard Educational Review* on the numerous reports that followed *A Nation at Risk*, Harold Howe II suggested that it was "doubtful that American education has ever before received such a concentrated barrage of criticism and free advice as it has in 1983."[3] Governmental and media attention to public schools continued into the latter half of the decade, with a new round of reports initiating a second wave of reform.[4] Reformers' original concern, student achievement, measured by standardized tests, soon shifted to discussion about the quality of teachers and their preparation, which became the "dominant conversation about educational reform."[5]

For the most part, discourse did not directly address the special needs of urban schools or their students, nor particular skills and attitudes that urban teachers of disadvantaged students should acquire. There were, however, two significant exceptions to the dominant conversation. One was the "emancipatory" perspective that developed in curriculum studies; the other emerged from efforts to develop an "ecological" approach to urban school reform.

Though some analysts saw a "bewildering array of policy initiatives" resulting from state efforts to improve the schools, the reforms of both waves shared several characteristics and assumptions that had important implications for urban teacher preparation.[6] Neither the problems of urban schools nor the reforms' effects on at-risk students were integral parts of the debate on improving public education, although some educators charged that the reforms enacted would erode any success that had been made in boosting academic achievement of poor, minority students.

EDUCATION AND THE ECONOMY

The causal relationship between improving education and rescuing the economy was emphatic in *A Nation at Risk*, which prophesied second-class status for the nation if its second-rate schools could not be made excellent. Most of the subsequent national reports similarly conflated economic revitalization with educational reform, including the Carnegie Task Force on Teaching as a Profession, a "second wave" document.[7] The Carnegie report, *A Nation Prepared: Teachers for the Twenty-first Century*, offered this rationale for educational reform:

> As jobs requiring little skill are automated or go offshore, and demand increases for the highly skilled, the pool of educated and skilled people grows smaller and the backwater of the unemployable rises. . . . As in past crises, Americans turn to education. They rightly demand an improved supply of young people with the knowledge, the spirit, the stamina and the skills to make the nation fully competitive—in industry, in commerce, in social justice and progress, and, not least, in the ideas that safeguard a free society.[8]

Later in its report the Carnegie Task Force reiterated the urgency of schooling's economic imperatives, identifying its concerns with those sounded by earlier reports, from the Education Commission of the States, the President's Commission on Industrial Competitiveness, and the National Alliance of Business. Indeed, the Carnegie Task Force report on teaching described education itself as a financial investment, one with a need for "improving the rate of return" and "capturing the benefits of productivity."[9] Some educators objected to the economic theory underlying this conflation of school improvement and economic competitiveness, as well as its political implications, which one writer charged represented "a retreat from democracy," but its pervasiveness was acknowledged by its sharpest critics, as well as its proponents.[10]

THE ASSUMPTIONS OF EXCELLENCE REFORMS

Without explicit reference to the compensatory programs begun in the 1960s or previous debate about the sources of disadvantagement, the excellence reforms took a position on both. The connection between poverty and academic success had been widely debated in the 1960s, but the excellence reforms reflected none of that controversy. They were emphatic in establishing cause-and-effect relationships between schooling and prosperity: Just as the nation's economic resurgence depended on technological innovations generated by an improved educational system, so the student's economic future depended entirely on acquisition of advanced skills.

Reform measures addressed first student and then teacher characteristics, rather than funding levels, institutional practices, societal conditions, or a combination of these. Robert Dreeban argued that a report issued by deans of the major schools of education, the report of the Holmes Group,

> takes on faith the primacy of teacher quality and fails to pose open questions about how curricular, instructional, and administrative considerations contribute to educational outcomes. . . . [It proceeds from] no analysis of schooling, of school system organization, or of teaching as an occupation.[11]

While the civil rights movement had aimed to use schooling to equalize social relations, to "democratize the competition" for economic success by providing minority students with the social and academic skills they needed to counteract racism's legacies, the excellence reforms looked to heighten competition, in school and the market. As the chairman of Xerox corporation, one of the most influential corporate leaders of the reform movement, wrote, "Competitiveness begins at school."[12]

Critics charged that increasing competition without providing more assistance to students who needed it would translate into greater educational inequalities. One critique of the excellence reforms argued that diverse reform measures "enacted in the name of excellence" from 1983 to 1986 often set

> new standards for achievement, but not new resources or strategies to ensure that all children will have the appropriate means to meet these standards. There are new tests for performance, but rarely new designs to create more responsive learning environments or to combat existing patterns of rigidity, inequity, and exclusion. . . . Such negligence is widening an alarming gap between the educational haves and have-nots.[13]

This "dark side of the excellence movement" would be especially gloomy for urban schools, because of the high percentage of students considered educational have-nots.[14] The demographic trend that began in the mid-1960s continued through the 1980s, with the central cities having an increased concentration of "older, poor, and non-white" residents.[15] Students from these populations were precisely the ones schools had been least successful in educating. In addition, one educator observed that their degree of disadvantagement had increased as well, as immigrants arrived from more impoverished regions of their own countries into the nation's cities.[16]

One of the few major reports to describe problems of urban schools, a report issued by the Carnegie Foundation for the Advancement of Teaching, warned that the students in urban schools were an "imperiled generation," and the excellence reforms were "irrelevant" to many of them.[17] Though this report emphasized that "excellence in education ultimately must be judged by what happens to the least advantaged students," it also accepted the economic rationale for the reforms, observing that the quality of education would determine "the vitality of our economy," adding to this economic imperative for reform the notion that reform would determine the "strength of our democracy" as well.[18] Like the reforms it faulted, this report made public education the key to national and urban renewal. In doing so it rejected arguments that many of the problems exhibited in urban school systems had to be addressed by slowing or reversing urban decay itself.[19]

The economic rationale for change influenced the locus of reform, as well as its content. Whereas school improvements 20 years earlier had concentrated on developmental issues raised in improving early education, the excellence reforms took up the demands of schooling's later years. This concern logically flowed from the new reform movement's raison d'etre, as explained in *A Nation at Risk*: providing students with the high level skills they and the country needed for ascendancy in world markets controlled by technological innovation rather than plentiful raw materials. The reform movement's pervasive economic rationale did little to encourage attention to the issues of schooling that dominate the early years.[20] Even sharp critics of the excellence reforms tended to examine issues of secondary schooling and curriculum independent from the problems of education in the student's first years of school.[21]

FEDERAL INVOLVEMENT AND FISCAL LIMITATIONS

Two critical changes in federal funding of education that occurred shortly before publication of *A Nation at Risk* also shaped the decade's discourse and reforms. In 1981 the federal government made "cuts and more cuts," causing educators to remember "the first six months of the Reagan administration as a period of fiscal disaster."[22] This "disaster" was followed by another seven years during which the Reagan administration "chipped away unrelentingly at federal aid to education."[23] The federal share of total expenditures for elementary and secondary education declined from 8.7% in 1980 to 6.2% in 1988, and total federal funding to elementary and secondary schools declined 26% during this period. Compensatory education lost 25% of its funding, which was a particularly heavy blow for urban school districts, especially in states that did not compensate for the decrease in federal expenditures.[24] One result of the chronic fiscal problems of urban schools was deterioration of school facilities, which had become so shabby, unsafe, and overcrowded, one author argued, that they manifested conditions that were prohibited by most municipal building codes for rental housing.[25] However, as in the previous decade, little attention was paid to the immediate or cumulative effects of funding cuts on teacher or student performance in urban classrooms.[26]

Perhaps as critical as the amount of aid the federal government gave to urban schools was the method of funding. In 1982 the federal government altered the system of contributing to state and local school systems, replacing many of the categorical aid programs of the 1960s and 1970s with block grants. By restricting how the money in categorical programs could be spent, the federal government had regulated change; by shifting the form of financial support to a general package of aid, cut loose from mandates about how it was to be spent, the federal government transferred its authority and power to control school reform to state and local authorities.[27] One policy analyst described the developments that began in the 1980s as a "counterrevolution in full swing."

> The Reagan administration, eager to return responsibility for education to the state and local levels, has condemned the recent federal presence as officious intermeddling. Because Washington lacks both the competence to set requirements [for school reform] and the capacity to carry them out, the argument runs, it should only provide education support (at levels markedly lower than those previously fixed), leaving decision making to those with a more nuanced understanding of the issues.[28]

In an analogous development, the Johnson era reliance on a prominent role for the federal government in prompting research and development in education was completely rejected in the 1980s, resulting in "federal fiscal starvation" of educational research.[29] One significant result of these alterations was that programs like TTT and the Teacher Corps, designed and funded by the federal government in the 1960s to improve preparation of teachers of disadvantaged students on a national scope, were virtually nonexistent.[30] To the extent that research and experiments in preparing teachers for urban schools were undertaken, the programs were small and local, in many cases funded by foundations, corporations, and individual universities. Even supporters of the primary national reform to emerge from a decade of reports and recommendations, a National Board for Professional Teaching Standards, struggled to gain just a portion of research and development expenses from the federal government, noting that the remaining costs would be matched by business executives.[31]

The push for educational reform at the state level often came from governors and business leaders, and it was "instrumentally linked" to the same issue that energized national reform: jobs and economic growth.[32] Though states adopted widely varying measures to improve their schools and their teachers, for the most part the state initiatives reflected the ideological underpinnings of *A Nation at Risk*.[33]

TEACHER QUALITY

The debate about teacher quality that characterized discourse during the 1980s contained little discussion about conditions of racial segregation or particular skills and attitudes teachers of disadvantaged students might need. One of the few writers to take up the issue of urban teacher preparation wrote that the major reports "pay lip service to the demographic dynamic" of increased numbers and concentrations of poor, minority students in urban school systems, but "have nothing substantive to say about preparing urban teachers."[34] Since little discussion occurred about any special problems urban school districts faced, by implication the same remedies for improving teacher quality could be applied to all school systems. Thus the dominant answer to the question of what skills or attitudes teachers of disadvantaged students in urban schools needed was that they required the same attributes and preparation as all other teachers.

Pointing to analyses of declining scores on a range of standardized tests, a stream of reports complained (usually in more subdued prose than the author quoted) that the country's "teaching corps is unacceptably incompetent" and that the nation could expect "only the numb and the dull to linger in teaching careers."[35] Not only was the "intellectual diminution of the cohort of available new teachers" a matter of great concern, but the best "are not being hired and the best of experienced teachers are leaving the schools."[36] To improve the quality of the teaching force, the reports converged in their recommendations to improve teacher preparation and professionalize the occupation.[37]

IMPROVING TEACHER PREPARATION

One author categorized the major proposals to reform teacher preparation into four models: one expanded the content of teacher preparation; another transferred responsibility for teaching teachers to master teachers in schools, an approach closely tied to demands for professionalizing teaching; a third model proposed changes that would take professional schools out of research institutions, making them like teaching hospitals; the fourth model suggested ways of spreading teaching of teaching to all university departments, eliminating separate schools and colleges of education.[38] As these categories indicate, none of the proposals directly addressed urban teacher preparation or the issues of teaching disadvantaged students, issues that dominated discussion about teacher preparation during the 1960s. Why?

One answer is that the excellence movement was fueled by concerns that displaced, even contradicted, the equity reforms of the 1960s. A nation at risk of becoming a second-rate economic and political power had less interest in children at risk. Furthermore, state initiatives aimed at raising exit requirements for students and entrance requirements for teachers were not balanced or counteracted by federal programs aimed at reducing educational inequalities. Another explanation is that discourse centered on individual characteristics of teachers or students, even when their collective attributes, such as declining performance on standardized tests, were examined. Whereas educational reforms two decades earlier had focused on group problems and characteristics — for instance, the special needs of poor, minority children — the debate over excellence took up national performance by way of individual achievement. Another explanation is that, as in the 1960s, a strong political current influenced scholarship and policy to locate the source of student failure in the students and their social milieu. The same kinds of arguments that had been advanced 30 years earlier by proponents of a culture of poverty were now presented by social scientists who argued that the nation's cities had produced an underclass that was beyond the reach of school reform.

The most prominent equity concern during the 1980s was the diminishing supply of black teachers.[39] However, debate over this problem also mirrored the assumptions of the excellence agenda. Many writers attributed the decline in the numbers of black teachers to the civil rights and women's movements, which, they argued, had opened up alternative careers for black college graduates. Thus education was losing black college graduates to more lucrative and higher-status careers because of the nation's success in eliminating barriers to minority students' academic achievement. However, Patricia Graham connected the decline to continued and greater problems in educational achievement for blacks, exemplified by a drop in the proportion of blacks attending college and those receiving master's degrees.[40] Perhaps more significant, discussion over how to recruit, attract, and retain black teachers followed the same contours as debate over the teaching corps in general, grounded in assumptions about the need for professionalizing teaching. While writers objected to competency tests which eliminated proportionately more minority candidates for entry into teaching, few questioned the absence of participation by parent or community groups in the process of determining selection requirements.

PARTNERSHIP VERSUS SERVICE DELIVERY

The proposals for reform of teacher preparation linked their measures to similar conceptions of the teacher's role. Their visions of the teacher's appropriate relationship to colleagues, administrators, and parents were derived from a "service delivery" model for education. They conceived of schooling as a service delivered to clients, that is, students, parents, and citizens, by professionally staffed bureaus—the school staff.[41] Service delivery conceptions of schooling have been used by educators concerned about equitable distribution of services, for instance, Ronald Edmonds, whose School Improvement Plan was based on a service delivery model.[42] However, some educators argued that by reducing both parents and citizens to client status, service delivery models encouraged polarization between client and provider, making families either victims or villains.[43] They proposed an alternative paradigm for analyzing public services such as schooling: to view parents, students, school staff, and community members as partners who shared responsibility for schooling's means and outcomes. This approach, which assumed that the teacher's professional authority was derived from the strength of the teacher–student–parent alliance, was variously labeled an "ecological," "holistic," or "partnership" concept. Although not identified as such, it was the theoretical underpinning for TTT's emphasis on parity, as discussed in Chapter 1.[44]

The ecological view of teacher preparation and school reform was implicitly rejected in the reports issued by the Carnegie Task Force on Teaching as a Profession, the Holmes Group, the American Association of Colleges for Teacher Education, and both teachers unions.[45] They all made teacher quality the linchpin of reform and, in so doing, rejected the importance of "properties of classes, schools, and school systems as they impinge on instruction."[46] The focus on teacher attributes encouraged, and was in turn fed by, the effort to professionalize teaching.

PROFESSIONALIZATION AND URBAN TEACHERS

The idea of a professionalized occupation has been debated among educators for a century and was not unique to this wave of reform. Lee Shulman's defense of teaching's claim to professional status was not very much different from the explanation Harvard proferred for creating its School of Education over 100 years earlier.[47] Shulman argued that

> The standards by which the education and performance of teachers must be judged can be raised and more clearly articulated . . . [through use of teaching's] knowledge base . . . a codified or codifiable aggregation of knowledge, skill, understanding, and technology, of ethics and disposition, of collective responsibility.[48]

Even what arguably became the most politically popular proposal, to create a national board to certify teachers and develop teaching standards and norms, a body that would be independent of local government, local schools, and institutions of higher learning, was not new.[49] Albert Shanker advocated such a national board, shortly after the Ocean Hill–Brownsville strike, as an alternative to allowing local school boards to set standards for hiring and performance.[50]

In contrast to the 1960s and 1970s reforms, this drive to professionalize teaching virtually dominated discourse about teacher preparation and school reform. Improvement of teaching was the critical element in the promotion of educational excellence throughout the states, and professionalization, in turn, was accepted as the solution to better teaching.

> Professionalism also implies a new social contract: the replacement of bureaucratic accountability with professional responsibility, with teachers themselves setting standards. . . . Professional standards rest ultimately in attitudes, beliefs, and actions of teachers.[51]

In the professionalization model, the teacher's professional authority replaced bureaucratic control of schools; but both models were based on the service delivery paradigm, deriving the teacher's authority

from special or superior knowledge. Both underscored the distance between the expert deliverers of a service and their clients. On occasion,
educators who supported efforts to professionalize teaching attempted
to redefine professional responsibility, to reconcile it with ideas about
schooling's broader democratic purposes. For instance, Patricia Graham
argued that

> We Americans . . . need to come to fundamental agreement about
> what we want our schools to do. In reaching that agreement, one
> group of Americans has a particular responsibility, though not an
> exclusive one, to participate in that discussion. They are professional
> educators.[52]

Such cautions about the political implications of professionalization
were rare among its supporters, however, and discourse about the need
to professionalize teaching generally compared teaching with law,
medicine, or architecture.[53]

Most of the literature on professionalization concurred that two
characteristics distinguished a profession: control over working conditions and over entry into the occupation. Teachers' powerlessness was
generally attributed to schooling's bureaucratic conditions, and in connecting recruitment and retention of high-quality teacher candidates,
discourse about teacher preparation became inextricably connected to
examination of conditions in schools.[54] However, the service model concept of professionalization implied one analysis of teaching's problems,
and the ecological perspective quite another.

TEACHING CONDITIONS

In accepting the service delivery model of education, supporters of
professionalization tended to analyze the structural characteristics of
schools that were barriers to teachers delivering appropriate services.
One widespread solution was "shared governance," which generally
included some form of parent participation, but in an auxiliary role.[55]
A related idea, "differentiated staffing," confirmed the client status of
parents and students and introduced new layers of salary and authority
in teaching. For example, *A Nation Prepared* argued that school systems based on bureaucratic authority should be "replaced by schools
in which authority is grounded in the professional competence of the
teacher."[56] Parents would not be involved in establishing standards for

teaching or school goals, which were to be set by the state and district. Teachers would meet with parents to try to adjust what the parents want to state objectives, but parental wishes would probably carry very little weight when compared with state requirements, because teachers' salaries would be keyed to their students' fulfillment of state standards.

The Holmes Group proposed a different relationship between parents and teachers, one that would make parents, as well as many teachers, clients. Only an instructor certified as a "professional teacher" could be a "child advocate" or could "speak with legitimate authority" to school experts, like psychologists and reading specialists.[57]

The designs to reform teacher preparation and schools differed in important aspects but all of them argued for professionalizing teaching by introducing a different division of labor into the occupation, reinforcing a client–provider relationship between teachers and parents, and assigning educators exclusive control over entry into the profession.[58]

Tomorrow's Teachers proposed an academic model to differentiate in both salary and responsibilities between "instructors" at the bottom of the ladder, "professional teachers" on the next rung, and "career professionals" at the top. *A Nation Prepared* suggested four tiers, ranging from "licensed teachers," to "certified teachers," to "advanced certificate holders," and at the top "lead teachers." The National Commission for Excellence in Teacher Education, issuing a report for the American Association of Colleges for Teacher Education, supported the concept of differentiation in general but did not outline one specific plan.[59] The AFT recommended two tiers, with "instructors," recent college graduates with no pedagogical training, performing less skilled labor and "career teachers" handling the tasks that require greater expertise. In addition, some career teachers would train interns and be given the status of faculty at cooperating universities or colleges.[60] The AFT proposal, perhaps reflecting the union's traditional rejection of reforms that linked pay to the quality of a teacher's performance, made no mention of differentiation in pay or benefits for instructors and career teachers.

Mary Anne Raywid's critique of the Holmes Group report could be applied to all the proposals for differentiated staffing. Raywid argued that

> Instructors have virtually no autonomy. . . . Professional Teachers will be permitted to run their own classrooms, but denied input to school policymaking; only Career Professionals will be both autonomous professionals and decision participants. The division manages

the job of splitting up teacher-related functions into three distinct levels of role and status, but it does so at the cost of denying to the two lower levels functions essential to maximal performance![61]

One of the dominant criticisms of proposals to create career ladders was that they introduced another layer of hierarchy into schools. Robert Dreeban argued that the Holmes Group's career professionals were administrators given another title.[62] Raywid observed that differentiation of responsibilities would probably be most effective if the divisions were not linked to hierarchies of pay and status. For instance, the help experienced teachers provided as mentors would "surely prove more welcome . . . if the roles were not formalized into two classes of citizens, with yet another tier of superordinates and subordinates."[63]

While critics of differentiated staffing argued against introducing pay and power differentials based on new job classifications, few analyzed the implications for urban teaching. If career ladders would "extend bureaucracy" by "making ever finer functional distinctions between and among school personnel," then they might be especially harmful in urban schools, which were already marked by a high degree of bureaucracy and hierarchy.[64]

Martin Haberman, one of the very few writers to relate the excellence reforms to specific problems in preparing teachers for urban schools, argued that the major reform proposals were irrelevant to improving urban schools. Instead, he contended, urban teaching required special training and a special license. Furthermore, urban teaching was so exhausting it demanded a "truncated career" of five to eight years; assumptions that urban teachers can maintain "lifetime careers at full tilt are superhuman, unrealistic expectations."[65] Haberman did not describe exactly how bureaucratic conditions in urban schools made teaching in them a special order of work, as he argued it was.[66]

Kenneth Tewel's portrait of how three principals responded to a crisis atmosphere in urban high schools illuminated those conditions. In Tewel's study, the schools' crises, manifested by widespread violence and disorder, encouraged principals to adopt a leadership style that was "hierarchical, authoritarian, excessively competitive, and ruinously uncommunicative." Each principal adopted an authoritarian attitude and maintained tight control over the change process. Each assumed a crisis mentality in which action to "save" the school took precedence over all else.[67] Tewel noted that the principals acted as they did because no institutional mechanisms constrained their intuitive behavior. How then would differentiated staffing have ameliorated the conditions that made the schools and principals susceptible to authoritarian practices?

If schools adopted some form of shared governance, as the major reports proposed, teachers would have been ensured an institutional role in deciding how to respond to the schools' crises. However, shared governance that placed parents and students in a peripheral role might well exacerbate the problems of urban schools. For instance, Vito Perrone, in a supplement to Boyer's *High School*, which examined four urban high schools, noted that they were struggling "for a consensus about purpose."[68] It seems unlikely that consensus could emerge without participation by all the schools' constituencies.

ECHOES OF EARLIER DISCOURSE

Reverberations of debates from 20 years earlier were still apparent in discourse about preparation of teachers of disadvantaged students. Perhaps most important, educators still struggled to define which students were disadvantaged, how, and why. One author noted that "things are much calmer on the educational disadvantagement front today—but that is not because the problems have been resolved. Rather, practically everyone now avoids the issue."[69]

However, a new explanation and a new term, *at risk*, emerged during this period. Instead of describing students' attributes, some educators noted that "certain large, demographically-identifiable groups gain significantly less than others from public schooling."[70] This new definition of disadvantagement signaled wider acceptance, at least among educators, of an explanation that made the fit between students and schooling the critical factor in school failure. This definition rejected both the student-deficit and the teacher-deficit models, generating a new concept of students at risk.

"At risk" meant failing to complete an education with an adequate level of skills.[71] Others defined students as at risk when schooling failed to provide them with the skills they needed to survive in the work force and be informed, active citizens.[72] One definition described at-risk students solely in demographic terms, noting that a large portion are from poor families of all races, minority and immigrant children, females, and children with handicaps.[73] Another writer employed the term *educationally disadvantaged* but combined the demographic and outcome descriptions generally used by writers using the term *at risk*.

> [Educationally disadvantaged students] lack the home and community resources to benefit from conventional schooling practices. Because of poverty, cultural differences, or linguistic differences, they

tend to have low academic achievement and experience a high secondary school drop-out rate. Typically, such students are heavily concentrated among minority groups, immigrants, non-English speaking families, economically disadvantaged populations.[74]

There was still disagreement about what caused the mismatch between students and schools, and here the old arguments about student and teacher deficits framed the discourse. Two writers argued that "too many teachers and principals are still unaware of the areas of conflict between the culture of the school and that of children raised in urban black communities."[75] One school improvement study in Chicago used James Coleman's distinction between families that were "structurally deficient" and those that were "functionally deficient" to examine school policy.[76] Still, the fact that the match between students and school had become the focus of debate encouraged more discussion of the problem in ecological rather than service delivery terms.[77] For instance, the previous authors concluded that school goals had to be negotiated with educators and parents to avoid the collision of school culture and black culture. Carl Grant's discussion of urban teaching reflected the same tension. He acknowledged the validity of arguments that urban teachers "are kept busy just trying to maintain their own professional sanity" and have neither the time nor energy to develop materials that would overcome the limitations of curricular mandates. However, he complained that "teachers rarely ask how, in spite of bureaucratic constraints, they themselves contribute to problems with the curriculum."[78]

CONCLUSIONS

The decade of reform that began with publication of *A Nation at Risk* focused public attention on education but the resulting changes did little to improve education for disadvantaged students. The problems of funding and racial isolation that plagued city schools were not relieved by measures to achieve educational excellence.

However, the neglect of issues that were pivotal to improving education for disadvantaged students may also have allowed a less politically charged environment for debate, which permitted some consensus to develop about the sources of and solutions to disadvantagement.

Nonetheless, the shift to definitions of disadvantagement that emphasized the fit between students and schooling occurred within a larger discourse completely dominated by concerns that prevented any widespread reform based on this principle. First, the singular emphasis on schooling's economic purposes excluded debate about education's political and social role in a democracy, a discussion that would have necessitated a focus on students whom schools had historically served least successfully. Excellence and equity were very much counterposed, in practice if not in theory, and debate about teacher preparation reflected the ascendancy of excellence reforms.

Second, debate about school improvement included reference to conditions of work, a development that could have encouraged attention to systemic characteristics of urban schools that undercut student and teacher performance. But this valuable insight was overshadowed by the prevailing strategy of professionalizing teaching. In accepting this framework for analyzing the teacher's relationship to parents, students, and citizens, educators accepted a paradigm for school reform that contradicted the benefit of including school conditions in the discourse about improving achievement of at-risk students. It further counteracted the other significant development in debate, adoption of the at-risk label for students previously identified as culturally deprived.

Thirty Years of Research

In Chapters 1–3 I have traced the answers educators have given in the past 30 years to four questions that underlie programs to prepare teachers of at-risk students in urban schools: What skills and attitudes do teachers need to be successful? How should preparation programs teach these skills? How do characteristics of urban school systems affect teacher performance? How should these characteristics be used to reform preparation of urban teachers?

SUMMARIZING THE FINDINGS

When an ecological perspective is used to analyze research over the past 30 years, the scholarship yields no conclusive answers to questions about specific skills and attitudes urban teachers of at-risk students require. Moreover, the scholarship itself presents a compelling argument for rejecting its quest for prescriptions. Because educators have disagreed about the sources of academic failure, they have reached no consensus about needed correctives in teacher preparation. Because the issue of disadvantagement has evoked what are essentially political disputes about the purposes of education in a democratic society, research has not provided solutions to the controversy. In attempting to generate descriptions of skills and attitudes that teachers required, researchers remained divided over the definition and source of academic failure. To a great extent, their political orientations framed how they would describe the reasons poor, minority children, labeled "deprived," "disadvantaged," or "at risk," fared poorly in urban schools.

Understanding the futility of combing research findings for a comprehensive list of appropriate skills and attitudes for teachers of at-risk students in urban schools is critical, for in rejecting the search for static, prescriptive answers, scholars can introduce a different framework, one that includes the social context of urban education.

In each of the three periods, shifts in the political climate framed the dominant reforms for preparing teachers of deprived, disadvantaged, or at-risk students. Yet since the early 1970s scholars have failed to address this broader context. Just as the political tensions of the 1960s charged public and scholarly discourse, sharply polarizing debate between advocates and opponents of theories of cultural deprivation, so the altered political environment of the past two decades has shaped answers to problems in urban schooling and in preparing teachers of poor, minority students. However, with the exception of a small group that has advocated a change agent approach, teacher educators during the past two decades have not given the political impetus for pedagogical change the attention it deserves.

For example, few writers have explored how changes in funding formulas and expenditures have altered instructional practices, or how the failure to racially integrate urban schools has changed educational outcomes. Perhaps the most dramatic example of both the impact of a changed political atmosphere and the unacknowledged scholarly accommodation to the shift was the rapidity with which educators began to describe urban school populations as "multicultural," a label that ignored the absence of white students in urban school systems as well as the defeat of efforts for racial integration.

POLITICS, POLICY, AND RESEARCH

The interplay between educators' political thinking, the political landscape, and research is complex, and the thorough analysis it deserves goes beyond my purposes in this book. But the effects of policy changes and alterations in funding of research are quite recognizable in research over the past three decades, starting in the 1960s, when the civil rights movement exerted enough political pressure to push through legislation addressing the academic underachievement of poor, black children.

Compensatory programs, which were a key ingredient of the War on Poverty, were based on the belief that the causes of academic failure could be readily identified and remediated by special programs for the targeted populations. This belief was held by many researchers, but, just as important, it was the basis of much federal and private funding for scholarship. Educators and scholars are researchers, and their thinking is influenced by turns of politics, just as public policy is. In addition, their scholarship is also framed by the opportunities they are given to conduct studies; they are encouraged and limited by the kinds of programs the government and private sources, like foundations or corporations, create and evaluate.

Compensatory programs were a double-edged sword, because while they acknowledged that correctives were needed to make public education serve its social mission, they pinpointed blame for academic failure on discrete elements, usually students or their families. On the one hand, the new programs, designed to give students additional assistance and materials, offered educators and researchers new opportunities to help poor, minority children. On the other hand, the programs, though they channeled additional money to urban schools, did not contribute the vast sums needed to make the reforms effective, and, to some critics, were ill-conceived, because they did not address the systemic causes of school failure. Scholars, no less than teachers and civil rights activists, were caught in this bind, but their research seldom addressed the dilemma explicitly. Most scholarship of the 1960s on improving achievement of disadvantaged students accepted the narrow boundaries established by the public policy of creating compensatory programs, and, with it, an input/output research methodology that severely restricted inputs considered relevant.

The compensatory programs represented a victory for the civil rights movement, but it was a victory that had to be expanded upon to validate itself. As David Cohen noted in his analysis of the More Effective Schools (MES) controversy in New York City, compensatory programs had to be vastly enlarged to give poor, minority students an education equivalent to the one their white peers were receiving in suburban schools. However, the disintegration of the social commitment to integrate urban schools made the prospects for increased funding for these programs dismal. This viewpoint, which became known as the "hostage theory" of school integration because it posited that urban schools would receive the funding they needed only if white students were kept there by force of law, became the last-ditch defense of busing and school integration during acrimonious feuds in the 1970s. When public opinion turned against forced busing and school integration, opportunities to study desegregation and integration also diminished. Subsequently, one factor in academic success, the effects of a racially integrated student population, has been omitted in much research on student achievement in urban schools. In fact, the Edmonds-inspired effective schools reforms and their substantiating research assume that significant school improvement is possible without changing the racial composition of classrooms and without increasing the amount of money schools receive.

Even if the effective schools strategy is correct in these assumptions, it seems obvious that the nature of the student population would be an important factor in a student teacher's urban field experience. Segregated schools generate special problems for student teachers, regardless of their race, because the racial exclusivity is a key element in the school culture, even if it is an unspoken one. Yet, research throughout the 1970s and 1980s, even that which advocated preparing urban teachers for a diverse student body or defended the need for multicultural training, consistently omitted reference to the departure of white students from public schools in urban systems and the ways this development affected urban schooling.

No body of scholarship yet exists that connects student and teacher performance to systemic characteristics of urban schools. No sustained or systematic debate about urban school effects on teacher and student performance has transpired. While many programs to prepare urban teachers in the 1960s contained *implicit* theories about the relationship between systemic conditions in urban schools and teacher education, lack of *explicit* discussion or analysis of this framework obscured their embedded assumptions. This was true even of Trainers of Teacher Trainers (TTT), which with its principle of parity among education constituencies insisted that responsibility for educational reform be a shared undertaking. Implied in parity was the assumption that school failure could not be attributed to an isolated characteristic of the college, school, family, teacher, or student; but how these components interacted and what caused dysfunction among them were issues that TTT did not address. TTT, like the Teacher Corps, remained locked in a framework that tried to solve the academic problems of poor, minority students without analyzing the characteristics of the urban school systems charged with teaching them.

Indeed, for the most part, educators have failed to apply social science research about characteristics of urban school systems to teacher preparation. This has in part been due to the hegemony of a paradigm that analyzes student and teacher performance, and consequently teacher preparation, without reference to broader political, social, and economic developments or conditions in schools. The research paradigm mirrors the preponderance of public policies that deal with educational and economic success as stemming from individual efforts and abilities.

Additionally, a good deal of the work purporting to examine life in urban classrooms has been personal narrative that relies on a teacher-deficit paradigm for explaining student failure, in essence rejecting the dynamic interaction among teacher performance, student needs, and school conditions. The result has been that characteristics of urban school systems, like overregulation and standardization of curricula, well-documented in the 1960s, have been ignored in shaping urban teacher preparation. Except to the extent that change agent programs have made individual teachers responsible for ameliorating the problems, the constraints of teaching in the urban school setting generally have not been considered in urban teacher preparation.

Two other factors help explain the emergence and resilience of approaches to urban teacher preparation that ignore the interaction of school, home, and political influences on teacher and student achievement. As Marilyn Cochran-Smith and Susan Lytle have written, the dominant paradigms in research on teaching over the past 20 years have excluded teachers' voices, questions, and interpretive frames. This conceptual oversight has been mirrored in the relatively scanty research about teaching as work, a topic that illuminates the conditions that influence urban teachers' performance. In 1973 Dan Lortie lamented the absence of such research, noting that the "most influential depictions of teaching in city schools are those of individuals who, having undertaken the experience, write exposes of what transpires there . . . a tradition which serves to generate blame rather than to explain recurrent patterns."[1]

The scarcity of scholarship about how conditions in urban schools alter instruction and learning reinforces the proclivity to study student failure using student- and teacher-deficit paradigms. Moreover, despite the small but growing number of studies about the school as a workplace, many researchers, even those using qualitative methods, continue to isolate their analyses of student performance from school characteristics. For example, Nancy L. Commins and Ofelia B. Miramontes conducted an ethnographic study of four low-achieving Hispanic students' language ability and use. They noted that the teacher made assignments with a skills-based orientation, devoid of any meaningful context, but they never connected their criticism of the teacher to a factor they identified but did not explore: Lessons were driven by the demands of district-mandated competency exams administered every 10 weeks. Their analysis of the teacher's behavior, his reliance on whole-class instruction, did not incorporate a theory of ways in which this behavior might be related to the district's rigid testing policy. Thus, they concluded that the problem was the teacher's underestimation of students' linguistic and academic abilities.[2]

Commins and Miramontes's work reveals how historic amnesia about research conducted in the 1960s encourages scholars to study the problems of at-risk students in urban schools using the same teacher-deficit paradigm, which has been virtually useless. In a study conducted 20 years earlier, five researchers, all former teachers in a large urban school system, observed four inner city junior high schools to determine how bureaucratic conditions altered teaching. They singled out the demands of external exams as a primary influence on urban teacher performance, and they documented how the lock-step curriculum dictated that children who were different in some way were treated in a custodial fashion, because they could not master the material in the same way and at the same pace as the curriculum demanded. The researchers catalogued how external examinations further diminished the teacher's ability to modify the curriculum, as well as the repercussions of adhering to it.[3]

To my knowledge, their findings have not been used as the basis for further research, but their conclusions were confirmed in a recent analysis of the ways teachers change what and how they teach when their students are measured by standardized achievement tests.[4] Researchers who questioned teachers found that the tests substantially reduced instructional time, narrowed what is taught, and encouraged teaching methods that were test-like and deskilled. This research, though not done in urban classrooms, challenges the assumptions and conclusions of work, like that of Commins and Miramontes, that locates academic failure only in the individual teacher's skills and attitudes.

In attempting to outline specific ways that teacher and student performance is changed by systemic conditions, researchers suggest a relationship among school conditions, teacher performance, and student achievement that complements the notion of ecological school reform. This line of research assumes that change in systemic and structural conditions in schools serving at-risk students must accompany or precede efforts to radically change teachers' interactions with students. Examining urban schools as systems contradicts the idea that teacher deficiencies or strengths can be separated from the conditions that encourage certain types of behavior in students, parents, and teachers.

Educators who attributed the poor achievement of at-risk students to school characteristics frequently acknowledged schooling's political context. However, historically they have tended to rely on solutions that are teacher-centric and neglect the disjuncture between home and school learning. For example, teacher unionism, at least in the form that became institutionalized, accepted the service delivery paradigm for school improvement, making parents and students clients and teachers service deliverers, rather than partners.[5] The various change agent strategies minimized or ignored parent and community involvement in school reform. Moreover, the strategy of preparing prospective classroom teachers to reform school structures demanded that teachers in the most pressed instructional circumstances become political organizers in addition to fulfilling their pedagogical responsibilities. As the

Teacher Corps experience demonstrated, change agent programs fail to recognize that the job of teaching in urban schools is so taxing that individual teachers, even those who are talented, fresh, and idealistic, cannot sustain the effort needed to make structural improvements in schools.

It is worth examining the reasons the change agent strategy became a popular method of urban school reform because it still drives much of the literature on teacher preparation that acknowledges schooling's political context. One curious aspect to the change agent perspective is that it emerged concurrently with unionization of urban teachers, and yet contradicted unionism's basic premise. If urban teachers had been persuaded that individuals could reform schools, then teacher unionism would not have mushroomed, for it relied on the belief that institutional change depended on collective activity. In voting to have unions represent them, urban teachers rejected the individualistic view of reform proposed by educators who argued for preparing teachers to be change agents.

In her review of two magazines critical of schooling, Maxine Greene noted a dichotomy between them, which she argued represented an unfortunate split in the progressive movement in education. One side, symbolized by a publication of the American Federation of Teachers, defended quality education for all in institutional terms but said little about teachers' affective goals; the other side advocated school change but made "the self-actualizing individual" its exclusive focus, rejecting any discussion of alternative institutional arrangements that would allow teachers to take up these values.[6] Greene's framework explains how the advocates of change agent programs, by making the individual teacher their focus, rejected teacher unionism's arguments about the need for collective action to force structural changes.

Scholarly neglect of the impact of underlying social and political conditions, like the state of the economy, on educational aspirations and achievement mirrors the ascendancy of political conservatism and the excellence reforms of the 1980s. The swath of reform proposals that warned that the nation's economic competitiveness and global strength were endangered by substandard public schools asserted a causal relationship between economic productivity and the educational system, which was asserted but not demonstrated. The "second wave" of reform in the 1980s, which was in part a response to the excellence reforms' neglect of equity concerns, did not challenge the economic assumptions of the excellence movement. Instead, these second wave proposals aimed to accomplish more effectively what the first wave of reform had begun, by embracing a strategy of professionalizing teaching.[7]

Ironically, the second wave of reform has also generated informative research about the school as a workplace, which reframes questions of teacher performance to take into account the relationship between school conditions and teacher–student interaction. Moreover, most scholars now use the label "at risk" to describe poor, minority students, demonstrating that they are at the very least sensitive to the controversy about the reasons for academic failure. This semantic shift to the term *at risk* signals wider acceptance, at least among educators, of theories that reject the either/or dichotomy of teacher- and student-deficit models to explain school failure. Unfortunately, the change may have been eased by the extent to which urban schooling and at-risk students are peripheral policy concerns.

A RESEARCH AGENDA FOR THE 1990S

To create a body of literature that will be useful in preparing teachers of at-risk students, two interrelated spheres need exploration: the world outside of school and conditions within schools, or what some researchers refer to as "macro" and "micro" conditions. We need to have a far clearer sense of the ways contemporary economic and political considerations alter urban school systems and our study of them. Included in this broad topic are questions about the ways urban school systems allocate scarce resources and the effects that diminished funding has on urban programs and policies, as well as educational research and development on urban school concerns.

On an even broader scale, we need to explain how economic, social, and political factors like unemployment and racial discrimination in hiring practices affect schooling's ability to democratize competition in the labor market. While this kind of research has been done, most notably by Christopher Jencks and James Coleman, their studies are barren of insights about schooling because their research does not incorporate the explanations students, teachers, and parents offer for their behavior. Nor does it include factors like school culture and organization, which can ameliorate or exacerbate social and economic pressures.

In a second area, educators need to understand far more about the ways conditions in urban schools influence teachers' and students' attitudes, behavior, and interaction. Research in this sphere should be informed by the scholarship conducted in the 1960s about the characteristics of school bureaucracies. For example, how do the bureaucratic and hierarchical organizations that characterize urban school systems influence instruction and teacher–student relationships? How do racial isolation and the entrance of different minority groups change the ways teachers and students behave? How does a school's separation from parents and neighborhoods affect urban teachers' interaction with their students and the students' perception of the teachers?

The specific context in which urban education occurs is shaped by the confluence of a vast number of factors, including a community's political culture and a school's history, the racial and social composition of the school community, the student's and the teacher's gender, race, class, and personality. The kind of research that is required calls for a breadth and complexity that heretofore have not been demanded, and we should expect that research that attempts to include all these factors will not be as neat or polished as the tidy studies that located isolated factors that promoted academic success.

In the last years of the previous decade and in the first two of the 1990s, there has been an encouraging increase in the number of studies that locate the problems of urban schooling in its broad social context, seeking explanations for teacher and student actions in the conditions of schooling rather than in its constituencies. One of the most important of these is Michelle Fine's ethnography of dropouts from a New York City high school.[8] Fine's work stands out in part because so little scholarship in the past 15 years has critically examined the relationships between school and society and the cultural disjunctures between home and school, as they affect student and teacher performance in urban schools.[9] In examining the school from the inside out, trying to establish how teachers' and students' interactions are framed by school conditions, Fine's study identifies and attempts to explain how New York City Board of Education policies influence life in a New York City high school.

Fine demonstrates how the school's arcane operating procedures, seemingly unrelated to the ways teachers conduct their lessons, frame their decisions about what is possible for them and their students. In many ways, Fine's study complements David Rogers's analysis of how the New York City Board of Education's organizational structure impedes substantive reform and democratic control[10]; Fine examines how the delineation of private and public concerns in a New York City high school sabotages students' academic success. Both authors situate their work in the political climate of the day, which shapes public demands on schooling. Rogers's context was the civil rights movement's campaign to integrate the schools and the bureaucracy's lack of commitment to the goal; Fine's is the public expectation that urban schools can solve the problems of unemployment and poverty within the existing framework of what is an appropriate concern for an urban school.

The paucity of qualitative research like that done by Signithia Fordham and John Ogbu, which traces the academic trajectory of at-risk students to determine who is poorly served by urban schools and why, is striking.[11] Fordham and Ogbu examine students' academic performance, tracing its roots in family and community culture and expectations, but analyzing how broad social conditions have in turn shaped these expectations. Their work focuses more on the micro experience but places it within the context of macro conditions, and like Fine, Fordham and Ogbu use qualitative methods to explain why students act as they do.

As noted earlier, the decline in attention to urban schools began in the mid-1970s, but the impoverished state of qualitative research on at-risk students is connected to broader developments in the social sciences. Micaela DiLeonardo explained the changes this way:

> Ethnographers fled American inner cities. In part it was the new dearth of jobs and grants for those doing anthropological work in the United States, in part a white response to race-nationalist hostility (only Xs should study Xs), in part the mass movement of black anthropologists to Caribbean and African work and of minority scholars in general away from social science to literary studies. Those who continued laboring in urban ethnography were less published, less reviewed, no longer newsworthy.[12]

Some valuable studies have been conducted about the relationship between school organization and student achievement and about the correlation between students' self-esteem and their academic success, but this research generally ignores the *interconnectedness* of teacher behavior, student performance, and school characteristics. While the research is helpful in understanding the effects of school and social conditions on student achievement, it does not illuminate how teacher–student *interaction* relates to school characteristics. For instance, Jeannie Oakes's study on secondary school tracking documents the effects of ability grouping but does not analyze why teachers and students behave as they do within the tracks.[13] Hence it lends itself to policies and further research that focus single-mindedly on teacher characteristics, for instance, on raising teachers' expectations for student performance. More useful research will uncover how educational practices, such as ability grouping, or organizational aspects, such as departmental divisions, influence the way teachers present material and relate to students. Understanding how these policies and the conditions they encourage frame teaching and learning should be the starting point of a body of literature.

More and more, schools in suburbs and rural communities have acquired characteristics that were unique to urban schools 30 years ago. Even small school systems, which 20 years ago were relatively homogeneous, are now ethnically diverse, and in accepting federal and state funds to establish special programs, school systems have created new layers of administration to implement and oversee them. Because most schools share a similar pattern of organization and administration, research conducted in a suburban school can be a starting point for understanding urban school conditions; but it is only a starting point, because the difference in scale generates qualitatively different problems for urban schools.

LOCAL KNOWLEDGE AND EDUCATIONAL RESEARCH

Acquiring information about the social context depends on researchers' interest in and ability to question and listen to urban teachers, students, and parents. As Claude Goldenberg and Ronald Gallimore have argued recently, direct experience produces the "local knowledge" that is needed along with the "propositional knowledge" of scholars. Local knowledge provides information on the cultural context, and that allows researchers to make effective use of their propositional knowledge.[14] As local knowledge is incorporated into propositional knowledge, researchers can begin their investigations with some understanding of how systemic characteristics of urban schools influence teachers and students.

Researchers need to have both an understanding of the breadth of conditions that influence school success and a methodology that is appropriate to analyzing the social conditions of urban schooling. Most educational research still shares with policy a proclivity for locating problems and solutions in individual performance, and scholarship that does not decontextualize student and teacher behavior is still the exception. So powerful is the ideology of individualism that it can undercut efforts of educators who consider themselves proponents of ecological school reform.

This process is well illustrated by Charles Payne's study that examined why some teachers in a Chicago high school were consistently more successful than others in gaining students' cooperation.[15] In his study Payne concurs with James Comer about the need for systemic reform, but his book shows that he has not taken into account local knowledge in designing his research. In failing to question teachers and school administrators in an effort to connect their actions to school policies, he ignores the array of bureaucratic procedures that influence how even mundane tasks are accomplished, or foiled, in an urban high school. Lacking this understanding, he is quick to pin the blame for students' misbehavior on individual teachers and to criticize their sloth and lack of concern. Although Payne agrees with Comer's perspective, his research violated one of the key elements of an ecological approach — disavowal of decontextualized individual characteristics as the cause of or solution for inadequate performance.

PROMISING BEGINNINGS

As researchers explore the interconnectedness of teachers' actions and working conditions, educators can begin to understand how factors other than student characteristics and teacher attitudes account for the custodial nature of much teaching in urban schools. Some of the most promising research compares achievement of at-risk students in urban and suburban schools, such as the study conducted by Rosenbaum, Kulieke, and Rubinowitz tracing the academic success of black children whose families participated in a residential suburban integration program and those in black urban neighborhoods.[16] Parents experienced suburban teachers as being more helpful — and more prejudiced than their urban counterparts. Suburban schools had higher standards for student achievement, but they also placed the low-income children in special education classes at a much higher rate. This study raises several critical questions about the ways suburban schools encourage or allow teachers to provide more assistance. It challenges the conclusions of studies undertaken in the 1960s that seemed to demonstrate that the teacher's racial attitudes were the key to academic success for poor, minority children, and it shifts attention to school conditions that should be changed.

Also illuminating is a study by Anthony S. Bryk and Yeow Meng Thum, which termed itself "an exploratory investigation" of how the structural and normative features of schools bear on the probability of dropping out and absenteeism.[17] They start from the premise that school organization plays a role in dropout rates and, using the strongest behavioral predictor of dropping out, absenteeism, compare organizational factors in public and Catholic schools.

The research promised by the National Center for Research on Teacher Learning (NCRTL) is exciting because it links what teachers need to learn about both subject matter and learners to the work environment.[18] Although NCRTL has not focused on urban schools, much of its research has direct application, and I use their findings on multicultural education in Chapter 6 when I analyze the kind of special preparation urban teachers need to deal with racial and ethnic differences.

Without acknowledging that characteristics of urban schools play a significant part in classroom life, we are hamstrung in preparing urban teachers for their job. Unfortunately, scholarly discourse in the 1960s, 1970s, and 1980s about preparing teachers of at-risk students in urban schools has, for the most part, failed to concede that we lack this understanding—and that we need to acquire it. There are indications that researchers are now more interested in using qualitative research to investigate how systemic characteristics of urban schools influence behavior. Without labeling their approach "ecological" or "holistic" they have adopted its perspective. Still, this research cannot yet be said to be a body of literature, because it has not generated a set of questions that need to be investigated, and thus research addresses important problems in isolation from one another. It is illuminating that the American Educational Research Association has a division for scholarship about the social context of education but no division or even special interest group for urban schooling, which could at least bring together researchers from other divisions and special interest groups to develop a common research agenda.

Understanding how urban school policies and the conditions they nurture influence teaching and learning should be the starting point of a body of literature. For that to occur, researchers need to reject the historic focus of most scholarship on individual characteristics of students and teachers, divorced from the social conditions of urban schools. However, they also need to draw together and draw on the newly emerging scholarship that is illuminating just how complex is the problem of preparing teachers of at-risk students in urban school.

Teacher Preparation
and Urban School Reform

One of the most striking aspects of literature on preparing teachers of at-risk students in urban schools is the boldness with which programs have presumed correlations between altering teacher preparation, improving urban schools, and brightening economic prospects for poor, minority students. Two major premises underlie most of the programs designed to prepare urban teachers of at-risk students in the past three decades. First, better schooling improves students' economic prospects. Second, teacher preparation can improve urban schools. The ideological assumptions embedded in these premises need scrutiny because they determine a program's choice of paradigm for urban school reform. The paradigm adopted frames the content and character of the training teacher-candidates receive.

In this chapter I first examine the political and economic assumptions of rationales to improve preparation of teachers of at-risk students in urban schools, analyzing what teacher preparation and urban school reform can be expected to accomplish. Then I discuss how these goals correspond to paradigms for school reform, including a service delivery model and an ecological approach.

EDUCATION AND ECONOMIC MOBILITY

Unfortunately, debate about the correlation between education and economic mobility has almost evaporated, displaced by consensus that the nation's competitiveness and each citizen's financial prospects are tied to schooling. The excellence reforms have been predicated on economic theories challenged in business publications far more than in educational journals.[1] Work of economists and political scientists who dispute the causal link between education, the nation's productivity, and its global competitiveness, or between citizens' academic achievement and employability, is rarely acknowledged in contemporary conversation on improving urban schools. Similarly, debate among historians about the complex interaction between illiteracy, poverty, and criminality on the one hand, and ethnicity, class, and gender on the other, has not been reflected in major proposals to reform schools or teacher preparation in the past decade.[2]

Relatively few educators today question the economic theories underpinning the last decade's reforms; they use the rhetoric of the excellence proposals without analyzing their implications. Michelle Fine's ethnographic study of a New York City high school illuminates how complex the relationship between educational achievement and economic success is for poor, minority students, and therefore how misguided is the design of school reform or teacher preparation when it accepts the simplistic causation assumed in the excellence reforms.

Fine describes four categories of circumstances in which poor, minority students left their urban high school prior to graduation: Some failed to graduate because of family, economic, and social obligations; a small group left in protest, with a well-developed, negative critique of their schooling; a third group saw no hope for the future and hence no reason to remain in school; a fourth type of student was dropped from school rolls after long periods of absence and was "passively discharged."[3]

These categories reveal how schooling might mediate students' economic prospects, but only if urban schools dramatically change how they respond to at-risk students, bridging the gap between students' personal lives and school and addressing education's social context. For example, students who dropped out to provide their families with income would probably be helped very little by altered curricula and instructional strategies unless the new regimen included jobs that paid enough to satisfy students' financial obligations. Fine's data point to changes that contradict the service delivery model of urban school reform, changes that rely on an understanding that students' home lives must be connected to schooling in ways they and their families help determine. By excluding parents and students from major decision making about schooling's outcomes and procedures, the service delivery model of education and its corollary, professionalization of teaching, inhibit this necessary change.

The limitations of urban school reform as an instrument for expanding economic opportunity are revealed in the contrast between students who left school with a developed critique of their instruction and those who drifted away, dropped from school rolls for absenteeism. The small group who decided to leave before graduation, as a conscious protest against their instruction and school norms, would benefit from pedagogical reform that addressed their objections; but those who saw little reason to graduate because they doubted they would find good-paying jobs with or without a diploma would probably not be deterred from leaving school because of instructional improvements. For them, the critical factor was disbelief in schooling's practicality, and their incredulity was encouraged by the numbers of underemployed and unemployed adults they saw around them.[4] Ambivalent about the value of an education,

> these adolescents recognize that there are few jobs waiting — diploma or not. But they also realize that without a diploma "it's tough out here. After two weeks of looking for work I started watchin' the stories [soap operas]. They don't want a black girl with no degree for nothin' but Mikkie D's [McDonald's] or maybe some factory work. Not for me."[5]

Fine concluded that the students' "seemingly contradictory consciousness captures accurately the economic realities faced by poor and working-class black and Latin adolescents."[6] She argues that only schools that address the social reality prompting their ambivalence can hope to convince them to try to graduate, but this means rejecting the dominant theory that academic achievement by itself can alter historic disadvantagement and substituting for it a view of education's value that reflects students' economic reality.

David Cohen and Barbara Neufeld have argued that schooling matters for poor, minority students because improved education can democratize competition by giving all children the opportunity to acquire the skills and knowledge they need for more equal access to job opportunities. This concept of the relationship between urban school reform and social mobility acknowledges the economic arguments driving the "schools-don't-matter" critique but simultaneously employs educational reform as an important vehicle for challenging inequality. In this perspective, the critical role of education for at-risk students in urban schools is affirmed but circumscribed: Better education in our cities cannot abolish labor market tyrannies, but it can distribute them more evenly, challenging present social and economic inequalities, though not eliminating them.[7]

This conceptual framework for urban school reform, unlike the initial argument for compensatory programs and the rationale for the excellence reforms, affirms education's limited usefulness as an instrument for addressing social inequality as well as its political, non-economic functions. Urban schooling's mission does not end with its economic purposes, any more than it does in nonurban settings. A democratic society needs to prepare all young people for lives as productive and thoughtful citizens, and the decisions we make about how future citizens will be educated are among the most critical we make as a democratic society. Amy Gutmann, a philosopher, argues that an essential characteristic of democracy is that citizens deliberate on education to decide how the society should reproduce itself.[8]

Using teacher preparation to improve urban schools in order to increase social and economic equality makes sense only when we are clear that schooling by itself is insufficient as a policy instrument for securing economic equality, and when we recognize that school reforms must account for students' social needs. Improved urban schools can remedy some "risk" factors for poor, minority students, for instance, by bridging the gulf between home and school, but other perils for at-risk children that endanger their academic success are beyond the school's reach. Schools can provide the skills students need to be able to compete in the job market and to be citizens who know how to define and execute their social and political responsibilities; urban schools cannot, however, by themselves alter many of the external conditions that subvert students' economic and political progress.

ALTERNATIVE MODELS FOR SCHOOL REFORM AND TEACHER PREPARATION

Professionalization of teaching has exerted an ineluctable appeal for over 100 years, but since the 1980s it has been the most widely accepted elixir for curing school ills and has dominated discussion of school reform, even among educators who think that reforms must take into account school conditions. One important exception is the work of teacher educators in the field of curriculum studies who have advanced a strategy of "critical pedagogy" to prepare teachers to promote social change.

Critical Pedagogy: Its Roots and Implications

Critical pedagogy, although it uses a different label and vocabulary, in many ways resurrects the change agent approach from the 1960s in that it assigns educators the task of transforming society through their classroom function, either as teachers or teacher educators. Unlike previous change agent strategies, the contemporary versions say little about the teacher's responsibility to change school structures, though they focus on curricular change, as did their unac-knowledged precursors.[9] Like the advocates of the earlier change agent strategy, two leading theorists of a critical pedagogy, Peter McLaren and Henry Giroux, assign teachers and schools of education a political function that transcends classroom borders. Teachers are, for instance, to develop "organic links" with community agencies and help their students engage in political activity that would be emancipatory.[10] No-tably little about existing school organization is taken into account in educating teachers for "critical consciousness" or "emancipatory peda-gogy," different terms for the same phenomena in curriculum studies.[11]

This absence of attention to the school environment contrasts sharply with change agent proponents' earlier focus on preparing teachers to transform their schools by being school leaders. The new change agent strategists argue not for imposing an additional role but rather for transforming the teacher into a political leader, who would educate students to be "critical of the dominant culture that offers such a disa-bling mass education."[12] Although the professed aims of the excellence reformers and the advocates of a critical pedagogy for teacher educa-tion are diametrically opposed, both groups assign a preponderant role to education in altering the nation's economic and political future. In so doing they propose a scenario for both political and educational reform that excludes citizens who are not educators from shaping social change.

Many of the advocates of making teachers political catalysts base their understanding of this role on the work of Paulo Freire, so a cri-tique of their perspective calls for discussion of Freire's ideas. They echo his theory that teaching victims of social and economic inequality "implies a correct method of approaching reality in order to unveil it."[13] Freire's "correct method" is to "unveil oppression, committing oneself to its transformation," thus fusing the teacher's roles as educator and political activist.[14]

Curiously, although a critical pedagogy demands the fusion of poli-tics and education, advocates of the strategy for teacher preparation and school reform have not critiqued Freire's political thinking or ex-amined the historical precedents of this approach. This is a serious omission for educators who believe that politics and pedagogy are the same process, because many of ideas underlying Freire's and their own pedagogy might well be rejected by prospective teachers educated to this perspective, even those who view teaching as a way to ameliorate social injustice.

The most frequently cited of Freire's works, *Pedagogy of the Op-pressed*, identifies three revolutionary leaders who exemplified his thinking about the melding of politics and pedagogy: Mao Tse Tung, Che Guevara, and Fidel Castro. With the selection of these figures, Freire places himself in a political tradition broadly associated with communism, but he does not refer to Soviet communists or to early school reform in Soviet Russia, both of which were of great interest to progressive American educators in the 1920s and 1930s and generated much debate. Despite the absence of any specific reference to this body of work, by Freire or the proponents of his ideas, a comparison shows that Freire's formula for melding political activism and education closely resembles John Dewey's description of education's purpose in Russia in 1927.

Dewey wrote that in Russia, schooling's mission was to "counteract and transcend individualistic tendencies in society." This "single and comprehensive social purpose" guided "conscious control of every educational procedure" and distinguished Soviet schools from those of other nations, progressive schools included.[15] Dewey observed that while he personally found elements of propaganda obnoxious, all attempts at social control have aspects of propaganda.[16]

As Dewey's description shows, the contemporary advocates of a critical pedagogy are not the first teacher educators to call on schools of education to construct a more egalitarian society, nor is the dispute about the appropriate relationship between political change and teacher education a new one. However, critical pedagogy presumes a relationship between school reform and political activity that differs in an important aspect from the perspective of the reformers who admired school reforms in Soviet Russia, at least until the late 1920s.

Lenin and the Soviet educators who supported him deemed efforts to reform society through education as utopian, which in the political parlance of the early communist movement meant that it was a strategy that contradicted tactics that could yield important, immediate victories. As Dewey explained to American readers, the Soviet educators thought that fundamental social change could occur only through the activity of the working class and its organizations in seizing political power. After revolution, however, education became critical, as the center of gravity shifted from the conquest of power to "pacific cultural work."[17]

Freire and his supporters invert the relationship between political reform and educational change assumed by Lenin and supporters of early Soviet educational reforms. Proponents of critical pedagogy give teachers and teacher educators the political task that their predecessors presumed was the responsibility of the working class and its supporters. Thus for Freire and those who use his work as a starting point for teacher education, education is the primary vehicle for social transformation. Yet, this political strategy is not identified, nor is it debated when a critical pedagogy is proposed. Furthermore, in ignoring the historical roots of their perspective, teacher educators who propose reforms based on a critical pedagogy fail to analyze how their strategy would produce results that would differ, if indeed they believe they should, from the early Soviet reforms. When Soviet educators made teachers and schools vehicles for propaganda, they were confident they were strengthening social forces of emancipation. If advocates of a critical pedagogy are equally certain that their strategy of fusing political organizing with teaching and teacher education will be emancipatory, they need to explain why the results will differ from the Soviet experience.[18]

The New "Social-Reconstructionism"?

While noting their sympathy with critical pedagogy's emancipatory goals, Daniel Liston and Kenneth Zeichner encourage an alternate strategy: the moral education of prospective teachers, to help them know and understand students' perspectives, to examine how conditions in schools inhibit teachers' success, and to deliberate on educational goals of their own choosing.[19] Their perspective corresponds to the ideas Dewey advanced about developing the prospective teacher's ability to analyze *all* ideologies and the pedagogies derived from them. In contrast to writers who argue that individual teachers must be agents of political change, Liston and Zeichner contend, I think correctly, that examination of school conditions and the entire social context of schooling is essential for teacher preparation.[20]

This perspective focuses on developing the prospective teacher's ability to deliberate on the choices available in the school setting, recognizing that social conditions encourage some choices but restrict others. As Zeichner explains,

> We try to create the kind of learning environment where differences can emerge and people can express them. I would be uncomfortable if one conclusion emerged. I think people grow by being exposed to differences and I would want the kind of environment for reflection that would allow the expression of opposing views. We really do not want to indoctrinate our students with particular perspectives. . . . As long as they've gone through and debated . . . and attend to the quality of their own interactions with students, I would be satisfied — I guess. Even if they disagreed with my own position.[21]

By placing the prospective teacher's growth at the center of teacher education and affirming teacher preparation's political responsibilities as well, Liston and Zeichner create an irreconcilable tension, which they acknowledge. This conflict is the unavoidable product of their commitment to education's democratic purposes; in teacher preparation or education, in fact in any activity that adheres to democratic ideals, the tension exists. Individuals given the right to make decisions may not reach the same conclusions as those defending the right would like to see.

Unfortunately, in discussing teacher education's relationship to politics in their comprehensive study, *Teacher Education and the Social Conditions of Schooling*, Liston and Zeichner slightly blur their otherwise clear-cut commitment to education's democratic purposes and character. They identify a critical pedagogy and their own thinking with the "social-reconstructionist" tradition, which during the 1930s stressed the role of the school in building a new society that would be more equal and just.[22] When placing themselves within this current of educational reform, they take care to distinguish their viewpoint from the strategy of George Counts, the first and most prominent social-reconstructionist, who argued that teachers and teacher educators indoctrinate students to the values needed for constructing a new social order. However, Liston and Zeichner's linking their own work to the tradition that Counts began is problematic.

Liston and Zeichner do not compare Counts's conflation of political advocacy and teaching and the similar, or perhaps identical, strategy of critical pedagogy, but the similarity is striking. In identifying their viewpoint with a tradition of reform that includes Counts and advocates of a critical pedagogy, they saddle their perspective with a political philosophy quite at odds with their proposals for reforming teacher education by encouraging moral deliberation about education's democratic responsibilities.

Although Liston and Zeichner place their perspective within the social-reconstructionist tradition, I suggest it fits more comfortably within an ecological model of schooling and school reform. They share the ecological strategy of addressing the entire web of relations that contribute to school success, and they enhance the idea of ecological school reform by extending it in two ways. First, their work analyzes how teacher preparation fits into the web, and second, it extends the configuration to include underlying social, economic, and political conditions. As Zeichner explains,

> Despite the desirability of this idealized vision of a democratic school
> community in which all constituents have a respected voice in making

school policy, there is little hope of achieving this ideal without linking
this project to efforts in other spheres of society that are directed
toward the elimination of inequalities based on gender, race, social
class, sexual preference, physical conditions and so forth, no matter
how noble our intentions. We cannot create democratic school communities in an undemocratic society. We cannot build "tomorrow's
schools" in today's unequal society.[23]

Zeichner's objection to the social and political myopia that has
characterized many of the second wave reforms could also be made of
the ecological strategy, which does not include the kind of explicit
analysis Zeichner's own work on school reform and teacher education
contains. However, the excellence and second wave reforms of the
1980s, as well as the compensatory programs of the 1960s, wrenched
school reform from social conditions, while the ecological strategy in-
sists on locating reform in the social context of home, family, and community relations. Proponents of ecological reform have not included
underlying political and economic conditions in their analysis; but understanding school reform as an ecological process invites examination
of all factors and conditions that influence student and school success.
In fact, the logic of ecological school reform *demands* inclusion of underlying social problems, as compared with the political and economic
assumptions of the excellence, second wave, and compensatory reforms,
which discouraged their recognition.

Liston and Zeichner explain that they locate their thinking in the
tradition of social-reconstructionism because it alone

> gives much attention to the giving of reasons, the formation of pur-
> poses, and the examination of how the institutional, social, and politi-
> cal context affects the formation of those purposes or the framing
> of the reasons. Only the social-reconstructionist seriously attempts to
> situate educational action within a larger social and political con-
> text.[24]

One might argue that the ecological approach itself belongs in
the social-reconstructionist current of educational reform, although its
advocates do not present it this way. Answering this argument fully
requires a more detailed historical examination of social-reconstructionism, theories of educational reform, and their relationship to left-
wing politics than the focus of this study reasonably permits. However,
briefly put, I think the explanation is that the struggle to transform
society's political and economic relations, the struggle for socialism,
historically has contained two "souls," one democratic, the other authoritarian.[25] In its democratic version, the process of struggle is as

critical as its fruits because it forges new social relations and produces a clearer picture of what a different kind of society should look like and what must be done to achieve it. In its authoritarian "soul," socialism consists of a package of preordained ideas, imposed by some sort of intellectual, technological, or political elite.

Because the ecological approach to educational reform depends on the active participation of all constituencies to reorganize relations within the school community, it is essentially a strategy to make schools more democratic. Therefore, it has a closer affinity to the left's democratic "soul" than to its authoritarian competitor. Social-reconstructionism's character is much murkier, and at best has a divided nature.

The value of locating Liston and Zeichner's writing in the tradition of ecological reform is twofold. The ecological perspective offers a hospitable intellectual environment, one that is substantially improved by their insights on teacher education and the social conditions of schooling. The commitment to democracy that is essential to Liston and Zeichner's viewpoint would be clarified and enhanced by its alignment with ecological reform, which unlike social-reconstructionism presumes that school reform is a democratic process. Like proponents of a critical pedagogy and social-reconstructionism, Liston and Zeichner advance a critique of school reform and teacher education that takes up the interconnectedness of schooling and political change. However, what separates Liston and Zeichner's analysis from the others is their unequivocal commitment to democratic ideals, and because this commitment is the linchpin of their thinking, Liston and Zeichner's work belongs in the company of writing that shares the same commitment.

REPLACING THE SERVICE DELIVERY MODEL

Most models and metaphors for understanding what teachers do and how schools should be reformed focus on discrete aspects of teaching. Teachers have been analyzed as reflective practitioners, leaders, researchers, and managers, to name only a few of the paradigms, and each role has generated an agenda for changes in school organization. All of these metaphors have merit and describe some aspect of the teacher's work, but without recognition of teaching's social context, these metaphors obscure more than they illuminate. Indeed, these models distort our understanding of teaching and of needed reforms, to an increasing degree as the school setting increases constraints on the teacher's choices.[26] Thus in urban schools, where teachers and students have little control over their environment, the power of these models to explain how and why teachers behave is sharply limited.

The various metaphors that focus on discrete characteristics of teaching can be grouped together in a single paradigm that presents the teacher as expert, someone who possesses knowledge and ability beyond the evaluative capabilities of laypeople who require the expert's services.[27] This paradigm provides the intellectual rationale for the policy objective of professionalizing teaching, which dominated the second wave of reform in the 1980s and drives much of the current legislation aimed at improving schools. This most recent struggle to professionalize teaching has been waged on two fronts: changing teaching conditions and altering teacher preparation so that it conforms to the training and licensure of acknowledged professions, like architecture, medicine, and law.[28]

In contrast, another way of thinking about school reform and the teacher's relationship to parents, students, and citizens is to start with the characteristics of the *setting*. This entirely different frame compares urban teaching with other human services delivered in government bureaucracies, such as social work, police work, and sometimes medicine. Michael Lipsky does this in *Street-Level Bureaucracy*, arguing that individuals who deliver human services in public service bureaucracies, regardless of their occupation, face the same systemic barriers to job satisfaction. For instance, doctors in Veterans Administration hospitals and their patients confronted frustrations and dissatisfactions identical in type to those voiced by social workers and their clients.

Urban Teachers as Street-Level Bureaucrats

Lipsky maintains that the essential dilemma in improving the way services are delivered in a bureaucracy is finding a way to give "street-level bureaucrats" the discretion they need to accomplish their jobs and fulfill their aspirations, while simultaneously ensuring that all clients receive equal treatment, the litmus test of fairness for a bureaucracy.[29]

How valid is Lipsky's analysis of teachers as street-level bureaucrats when compared with the paradigm that views teachers as professionals? One gauge is whether studies of conditions in schools have supported his conclusions as they apply to teaching. For example, Lipsky argues that street-level bureaucrats experience alienation from their jobs in four ways, all of them stemming from unsatisfactory relationships with clients.

(1) They tend to work only on segments of the product of their work; (2) they do not control the outcome of their work; (3) they do not control the raw materials of their work; and (4) they do not control the pace of their work.[30]

Judith Warren Little's research on the conditions of teaching that contribute to collegiality supports Lipsky's first condition. Her analysis of the systemic conditions in schools that contribute to teachers' isolation from each other confirms the validity of Lipsky's contention that like other street-level bureaucrats teachers work in isolation from other teachers.[31] Rebecca Barr and Robert Dreeban's work analyzing how factors of school organization restricted teachers' instructional alternatives confirms Lipsky's third and fourth conditions.[32] They identify factors that make teaching more difficult, such as the large number of low-aptitude students in any one class, greatly reduces the teacher's available alternatives to unsatisfactory ones.

A study of working conditions in urban schools, conducted at the same time *A Nation at Risk* published, identified four "stressors" teachers experienced in six schools in two large cities; all were conditions over which teachers had no direct control but that influenced how well they felt they could do their jobs.[33] The study confirmed, at least for urban teachers, the sense of powerlessness Lipsky describes.

Lipsky notes the appeal of professionalization as a method of resolving the street-level bureaucrat's dilemma, but he argues that "the professional fix" only exacerbates the conflict, since it ignores "the great gap between the service orientation of professionals in theory and professional service orientations in practice."[34] He identifies three areas in which professionalism undercuts the ideals of service.

> First, professionals by definition are accountable only to peers . . . [which] insulates them from the criticism of clients and people who would speak on clients' behalf. . . . Of greater impact overall are informal peer pressures (as opposed to reviews) that guide professional development. . . . Untempered peer definition of professional norms thus effectively erodes the client orientation to which professionals are theoretically committed [and] the norms usually inhibit professionals from seeking guidance in solving problems or providing services to clients, since to ask for help would be to admit a degree of incapacity. . . . Third, the most powerful agent in professional socialization is the work setting. Thus it is the extremely rare newcomer who is able to assert unpopular or unsanctioned values.[35]

Finally, he argues that "the record of the professions suggests that the model they provide in practice is not necessarily an auspicious one for increasing responsiveness to clients."[36]

Lipsky's critique contradicts the assumptions and strategies of the major reforms of teacher preparation during the past 10 years. His most valuable insight is that teacher quality cannot be improved without examining relations between teachers and their clients, as well as the social and cultural values reinforced by the organization and delivery of services. In fact, by limiting parental participation, the professional fix ultimately heightens alienation, because teachers are cut off from their clients' own knowledge about their needs.

Although Lipsky uses the language of service delivery, his suggestions for reform parallel the ecological proposals of other writers addressing school improvement. The significant difference between Lipsky and educators who analyze school using an ecological approach derives from their varying specializations within the social sciences. Lipsky, a political scientist and policy analyst, emphasizes the broad, systemic characteristics of delivering human services in bureaucracies. James Comer, a psychiatrist, stresses the importance of understanding the social and psychological climate of schools. However, their work is mutually complementary, with Lipsky providing a sociological explanation for the problems of school climate that Comer details. Lipsky explains what Comer observes: that schools "cannot adjust easily to groups or individuals with needs different from those of the majority" because of their "hierarchical and authoritarian" organization.[37] Lipsky's analysis led him to conclude that clients had to become a more potent force in service delivery, and the deliverers of services had to educate clients to make better judgments about seeking service and assessing the service they received. Similarly, one of the key components in James Comer's School Development Plan is provision for parent education, as well as parent participation in determining schooling's objectives and means.[38]

JAMES COMER'S ECOLOGICAL APPROACH

Comer termed his School Development Plan an "ecological approach to intervention" because it analyzes student and school staff behavior as a function of both person and environment.[39] He argues that student learning in four environments affected teaching and learning in school: in the child's home; in the family's social network; in school; and within the larger society.[40] By weaving together all these factors in his explanation for the failure of poor, minority children in urban schools, Comer has fashioned a theory that bridges the "victim/villain" deficiency of the service delivery model. In emphasizing the school's ethos, as developed jointly by school staff and parents, Comer avoids the dichotomous explanations that focused either on teacher abilities or student characteristics, which were typical of much of the literature on teaching disadvantaged students. Furthermore, Comer is one of the few writers who, along with Frank Riessman, have analyzed the job of teaching disadvantaged students within the school organization, considering how the culture and characteristics of schools cause their failure to adjust to students' human needs.

> For this reason, children from families under stress, children who are underdeveloped, or those who are less likely to learn and behave as expected are at greater risk in the school structure. The sources of risk are *in* the schools, as well as in societal and family conditions outside the school.[41]

Comer argues that all aspects of school functioning must be part of an ecological approach to educational improvement, including curriculum planning, social and psychological services, extracurricular activities, classroom management, and the many personal interactions that occur between and among staff, parents, and students on a daily basis.[42] Good people, superior teaching strategies, innovations, and materials will be ineffective in a "confusing, chaotic school climate where the staff is unhappy, isolated, and overwhelmed."[43] Comer explicitly counterposes his theory of school reform to the effective schools approach, noting that the "consideration given to climate is really only superficial in the sense that only such surface operations as discipline and rules are emphasized but not deeper and more basic concerns such as school organization, decision sharing and parental involvement."[44]

Comer's Program for Teacher Preparation

Comer's work shares a focus on child development with many projects that, like his New Haven program, began in the 1960s; but unlike many contemporaneous projects, Comer's program continued for more than seven years. His thinking about teacher preparation evidently developed from his project experience, especially the first year, which by his own admission was less than successful. Comer describes the project's history in *School Power* but does not explain how his ideas about teaching disadvantaged students or preparing their teachers evolved over the years in response to the program's strengths and deficiencies. Therefore, it is informative to compare Comer's account with one given by Roland Barth, who served as a school principal in the program's troubled first year. Unlike Comer's description, Barth's study analyzed the project's failures from inception through its first year, suggesting what lessons should be drawn from the experience.[45]

Comer's own description of disputes among the young, idealistic, newly minted teachers who were recruited to the project, the veteran teachers, and parents illuminates that the program was conceived without a philosophy of education, an observation that Barth makes as well. What is clear from Comer's account in *School Power* is that he gradually learned that an experiential approach to schooling, like the one John Dewey advocated, best complemented his thinking about the centrality of the child's psychological and social development to learning. Ironically, the teachers who were initially invited to teach in the project schools but were fired after the first year held this philosophy; the older, more experienced teachers, whose traditional teaching styles and values parents approved of, had to learn these techniques from curriculum specialists.

School Power outlines a program of teacher preparation that Comer has more or less repeated in subsequent publications. Its essential elements are "in-depth training in child development, supervised exposure to children in schools for several years, and career guidance before beginning to work as full-time, licensed teachers in school."[46] In the project's first year, most of the new teachers lacked these characteristics, so Comer evidently learned from that experience, although *School Power* notes no connection between the kinds of teachers recruited for the project initially, their disastrous experience, and Comer's subsequent ideas about teacher preparation. However, Barth describes the teachers as "inappropriately trained or inappropriately selected (or both)" and explains what he learned about teacher preparation.[47]

Unfortunately, *School Power* contains no discussion of the process the project members or director used to build on successful arrangements or eliminate problematic practices.[48] Therefore, it is not possible to know why Comer's current prescription for teacher preparation duplicates an aspect of the original plan that apparently, from Comer's own account, was flawed. However, from his experience in the project, Barth concluded that teacher preparation could not assume that teachers would function in the ideal school environment.

> Those who would prepare teachers to change public schools do an irresponsible disservice to the teachers, their students, the parents of students, and the schools unless they acknowledge certain realities: teachers must be trained to teach as they will be expected to teach. Teachers, as part of their training, must have ample opportunity to experience the problems of the real world for which they are being prepared.[49]

Comer called for three major changes in teacher preparation. First, academic learning should be understood as a product of overall child development, not an isolated mechanical function. Second, school personnel needed training to develop "skills to create a school-relationship climate that promotes development and learning."[50] Third, school personnel should be selected for their capacities to work in a collaborative fashion. Comer maintained teachers had to be prepared to work collaboratively with support staff, such as school psychologists and social workers, who in his School Development Plan played a critical role as a mental health team. Teacher preparation had to help future teachers

> to understand how a power-sharing organizational structure and a collaborative management style, with strong administrative leadership, reduces parent and student distrust and alienation. They also need to know how to create and participate in this climate.[51]

Comer's plan would indeed prepare teachers for work in schools that were involved in his School Development Plan, but not in traditional urban schools. His course of study would probably be far less helpful, even counterproductive, for teachers whose first jobs would be in schools with none of the structural changes or supports the School Development Plan provided. For example, training to work collaboratively with school support personnel would be of little value to teachers in schools that had quite limited access to services of school social workers and psychologists. In fact, one might argue that teachers must acquire the ability to function *without* these services, despite the pressing need.

None of Comer's writing about teacher preparation directly addresses the issue of the role teachers should assume in inducing changes in school climate. He advises that preservice programs should teach prospective teachers how to create a different school environment, but he notes elsewhere that for his School Development Plan to be effective, school authorities must commit resources for a number of years, implying that it requires institutional support.[52] School people cannot "greatly modify . . . economic and social risk-producing factors," but he argues that they can change educational practice and policy. He does not, however, clarify what school people can or should do to effect school change in buildings that have not participated in a School Development Plan such as the one he proposed.[53]

APPLYING AN ECOLOGICAL APPROACH

If we reject the service delivery model as Lipsky proposes, as well as the revised change agent perspective advocated by proponents of a critical pedagogy, and Comer's formulas for teacher preparation, how can programs preparing urban teachers help to improve urban schools and academic prospects of at-risk students? Their primary goal should be teacher preparation, as I discuss in Chapter 6. However, programs of teacher preparation have an additional institutional responsibility to help reconstruct relationships among parents, teachers, students, and citizens. This transformation of relationships is essential if urban schools are to succeed where they have historically failed, because urban schools' inability to serve poor, minority students stems from the design adopted for them at the turn of the century.

As Carl Kaestle explains, bureaucracy and standardization in urban schooling developed in response to the political pressures exerted by the rapid expansion and diversification of the population in American cities. Whether bureaucracy and standardization in urban schools, as Kaestle argues, reflected the "school men's" sense of fairness and efficiency, or whether as Michael Katz maintains they were primarily techniques of political control,[54] there is little argument that they were politically motivated but had significant educational results.

> The dilemma of standardized impartiality and quality control through systematization is that the decision-making processes are taken out of the hands of the person who deals directly with the system's clients — the children — and therefore tends to depersonalize the relationship. The teacher becomes more a part of the apparatus and less able to be flexible. Also, to the extent that the system intentionally masks the identity of the student to ensure impartiality, the student loses part of his individuality. Formalized impartiality leads to anonymity.[55]

Urban school systems were designed to make education impersonal and inflexible, and therefore, the "school men" maintained, urban schools would treat everyone equally by treating them the same. David Cohen and Barbara Neufeld point out that this earlier definition of equality has been challenged by another that replaces equality of *condition* with equality of *opportunity*.[56] This new concept demands that schools adapt to students' circumstances, but the organizational structure of urban school systems and the relationships between education's constituencies that the structure engenders have not been altered. Historians disagree about the motives of "school men" at the turn of the century, but they accept that urban schools were by design insulated from the political pressures of poor and working class parents, and in being insulated from political challenges they were also cut off from parents' knowledge about students, as well as the possibilities of cooperation.

Teacher Preparation's Institutional Role

Just as individual teachers cannot reform schools, teacher preparation cannot by itself reform urban school systems. As Larry Cuban argued in critiquing the Holmes Group plan, teacher preparation cannot substitute for the political and social *movements* that are needed to alter the systemic deficiencies of schools.[57] A program of teacher preparation can improve individual schools with which it is involved through its relationships with parents, community members, and liberal arts faculty, but it cannot alter the *systemic* characteristics of urban schools, especially those stemming from bureaucracy.

Cuban's assessment of the need for broader political forces to be brought to bear on school reform rested on the experiments with teacher preparation in the 1960s. Historical descriptions of the formation of urban systems indicate that the essential characteristics of urban school systems persist because their transformation requires a political and social movement that can overcome the forces of inertia that inhibit any change. The society as a whole must grapple with the contradictions that prompted urban "school men" to construct urban systems as they did. Unfortunately, contemporary discussion about teacher preparation and school reform barely acknowledges the political roots of standardization and bureaucracy, which now plague nonurban school districts as well, though to a lesser degree because the conditions encouraging and sustaining these practices are not as fully developed in nonurban areas.

By stressing the importance of developing new institutional relationships among liberal arts faculty, education faculty, schools, and community, Trainers of Teacher Trainers (TTT) attempted to counter the isolation between education's constituencies. This objective seemed to set a far more circumscribed role for teacher preparation than did the change agent programs, like the National Teacher Corps. Actually, TTT demanded more of teacher preparation programs, for it made schools of education the *institutional* vehicle for assisting urban schools to overcome the school–society and home–school disjunctures that sabotage achievement of at-risk students.

To the extent that change agent programs, as well as programs designed to correct teacher deficiencies in order to improve student achievement, designate the individual teacher as the key to improving urban schools, they relieve teacher preparation of any institutional involvement with urban schools. When colleges of education prepare teachers to be change agents who transmit the values and ideals of the teacher educators, the institutions neglect the more difficult task of reconciling the frequently contradictory demands made on education by community, teachers, parents, and students. That is, they dispense with TTT's goal of parity.

Each constituent in TTT's mission of parity represented a critical element for academic success. Parent participation addressed the conflict between school and home values; community representation was designed to bridge the school–society chasm that isolates urban schools from the social and political realities that so greatly influence academic achievement, as Ogbu and Fine demonstrated; the school staff's involvement with parents and citizens in implementing teacher preparation encourages the ecological changes within schools that Comer advocates, and accommodates variations in the culture of each school site. Thus the concept of parity makes the school of education a vehicle for urban school reform by using teacher preparation as an institutional catalyst.

One of the most widely discussed techniques for involving schools of education in school reform through programs of teacher preparation is the Professional Development School advocated by the Holmes Group. This strategy acknowledges the institutional responsibilities of schools of education to alter relationships among education's constituencies and will probably improve aspects of schooling for students and teachers directly served at each site. However, the strategy is flawed for a number of reasons beyond its reliance on the service delivery paradigm and professionalization, as I explain in Chapter 3.

First, there is no mention of a method to replicate accomplishments in other schools. As Larry Cuban argues, the Holmes Group report assumes that the Professional Development Schools will have a lighthouse effect, illuminating for others how to improve education. In reality, many of the achievements of these new lab schools will result from the direct involvement and resources of schools of education; to imply that other schools can apply these lessons without immediate support and participation by the school of education suggests few systemic conditions underlie problems in urban schools.

A second, related conceptual flaw is that the Professional Development School strategy does not take into account the political dimensions of conflicts in urban school reform or the role of higher education as a whole and liberal arts faculty in particular in shaping public policy and opinion. Teachers and teacher educators have a special role in debate about how urban schools can best serve their students, but so do liberal arts faculty. Determining what and how urban schools should teach entails a volatile discussion, as scholarship of the past 30 years demonstrates, but the debate must occur if urban schools are to win the confidence and participation of parents and citizens.

For example, one of the most pointed disputes that must be resolved is the issue of multiculturalism in designing curricula. While teachers and teacher educators have direct experience and certain kinds of information about the dispute, the matter directly concerns liberal arts faculty, as well as citizens. The Professional Development School makes schooling and school reform the domain of teacher preparation, and in doing so cuts off participation by citizens and the college community as a whole.

A carefully designed program of teacher preparation might bring the resources and expertise of teacher educators and liberal arts faculty to an urban school and, despite the worsened conditions, improve that particular school, as members of the Holmes Group and other universities have demonstrated in the past few years.[58] But success in establishing an institutional relationship with a school will be undercut when teacher educators bring a message of professionalization, for it contradicts the necessity for urban schools to bridge home–school and school–society chasms, as well as the gulf between practitioners and professors.

The kinds of arrangements that colleges can initiate to establish parity, as TTT's success demonstrated, will vary widely and depend on the resources and interests of each faculty. As I discuss at the conclusion of Chapter 1, many of the ideas that sparked enthusiasm at TTT sites deserve consideration today. When teacher-candidates must investigate the work of social service agencies in the cities where they will teach as part of their preparation, the goal of parity is being tackled. When education students tutor in urban community centers as part of their training, the college that organizes this field service acknowledges the importance of parity. When parents are involved in teacher preparation, as they were at the City College TTT project, prospective teachers learn first-hand about the benefits and difficulties of making parents partners.

Certainly, coursework must help prospective teachers understand why experiences like these are essential, why schools must be connected to the communities they purport to serve, and why teachers must know the value of involving parents in their children's schooling. That is, coursework that prospective students take as part of their preparation should explain and reinforce the character and rationale of the preparation they receive. Given this intellectual foundation, TTT's philosophical premise of parity should be the starting point for developing other methods of using teacher preparation as a vehicle for urban school reform. In the following chapter I outline what a program that uses TTT's commitment to parity would be like.

6

Preparing Teachers
for Urban Schools

By using the terms *urban* and *at risk* interchangeably to describe poor, minority children, scholars have confused discussion about what kind of special preparation urban teachers of at-risk students require. For example, the NDEA National Institute for Advanced Study in Teaching Disadvantaged Youth Task Force report, discussed in Chapter 1, rejected theories of cultural deprivation, and with them the idea that teachers of disadvantaged students required special preparation. However, the report noted that teachers in "deprived areas," like their students, "quit because they fail," primarily because of working conditions and student behavior.[1] In its failure to connect the organizational characteristics of urban schools to student and teacher failure, and in turn use this understanding to adapt teacher preparation, the Task Force report was no different from other scholarship of the period, or for that matter of the next 20 years.

Understanding the systemic sources of school failure is critical to transcending the debate over causes of disadvantagement, and applying these insights to teacher preparation is essential if urban teachers are to be prepared to adapt to their setting. Identification of decontextualized student, teacher, or parent characteristics that encourage academic success is a futile quest because the same attribute may be ineffectual or have a negative impact in different school settings. In addition, the search for these characteristics undermines efforts to understand how school settings influence teacher–student interaction and to encourage teachers to take them into consideration in devising teaching strategies. Finally, pinning school success on discrete characteristics of parents, teachers, or students is politically destructive because it encourages each party to blame the other for failure, rather than collaborating to understand and correct the conditions that make the school environment unrewarding for all involved.

This last factor may be the most valuable insight that James Comer's work has provided for urban teacher preparation. In starting from the political premise that all parties feel dissatisfaction when schools fail in their mission, Comer rules out the possibility that any one constituency will be blamed or changed in isolation from the others. This causes a parallel shift in the aims of urban teacher preparation, away from giving the prospective urban teacher knowledge about student characteristics or specific skills and attitudes to teach students effectively, which, as my literature review explains, has been the intent of most programs. In an ecological framework, what becomes most important is helping the prospective teacher understand how both the teacher's and student's aspirations, abilities, and knowledge can be used to overcome the common obstacles that urban school systems and social and economic forces set before them. Although they do not identify their perspective as ecological, the program of teacher preparation that Daniel Liston and Kenneth Zeichner have described in *Teacher Education and the Social Conditions of Schooling* uses an ecological approach, as I explain in Chapter 5.[2] It is in all respects of content and character the kind of program that urban teachers need, because it equips them to deal with the most salient characteristic of urban school systems, at least for the purposes of preparing teachers of at-risk students — the schools' systemic incapacity to accommodate *differences*, which is reinforced by their political insularity. Liston and Zeichner do not explicitly comment on urban teacher preparation, but because they have developed an outline for teacher education that takes up the social conditions that frame teachers' work, their framework accommodates urban teacher preparation with little modification.

In this final chapter, I describe the special requirements of urban teacher preparation and explain how Liston and Zeichner's work needs to be modified to make the fit even closer between their suggestions and the needs of prospective urban teachers.

DEALING WITH DIFFERENCES IN URBAN SCHOOLS

The recommendations in this chapter for preparing teachers of at-risk students in urban schools are based on the premise that urban school systems cannot adjust to differences in student learning styles, family cultures, and teacher strengths or weaknesses. Teachers work in isolation from the family and community resources that might help ameliorate the effects of the systemic incapacity to address individual needs. As historians of urban education have documented, the adoption of standard procedures and uniform performance measures to ensure impartiality produced urban school systems incapable of accommodating individual or group differences, indeed ideologically opposed to doing so. Furthermore, the bureaucracies that control urban schools were designed to be politically insulated from parents and communities, a legacy that makes collaboration and mutual assistance difficult if not impossible. Thus students' ability and proclivity to adapt to the behavioral or instructional norms dictated by highly regulated, inflexible curricula and policies frame their school success.

John Ogbu's work examining the reasons some minorities fare better academically than others, despite barriers of language and culture, confirms why the isolation and rigidity of urban schools are such critical factors, compounding the alienation and distrust that members of "involuntary minorities" experience outside the school walls.

> Since they do not trust the public schools and white people who control them, involuntary minorities are usually skeptical about whether the schools can educate their children well or not. . . . Another factor discouraging academic effort is that involuntary minorities – parents and students – tend to question school rules of behavior and standard practices rather than accept and follow them as the immigrants appear to do. Indeed, involuntary minorities not infrequently interpret the school rules and standard practices as an imposition of a white cultural frame of reference which does not necessarily meet their "real educational needs."[3]

The life experiences of poor, minority students who make up a majority of the student population in urban schools are a vital consideration in teacher preparation, but these experiences are most fruitfully analyzed when they are seen in relation to school characteristics, as John Ogbu's research demonstrates. Any search for decontextualized teacher abilities and aptitudes that promote school success for poor, minority students mirrors in method and outcome the historically fruitless quest to pinpoint how the culture of disadvantaged students and their families undercuts academic achievement. Yet, despite three decades of inconclusive and contradictory research using this paradigm, a large portion of the research conducted on underachieving and at-risk students still isolates individual traits or abilities, with no reference to the urban school context.

Over 20 years ago a report for the California State Department of Education concluded that there was no satisfactory answer to the question of whether "a unique set of personal characteristics and competencies are necessary for success as a teacher in a disadvantaged area school." Though correct, the report did not explain why the answer was elusive.[4] Examining research over the past three decades shows that no comprehensive answer is possible because the question calls for a generic prescription, a formula that denies the role of the school setting and its changing context. Indeed, the report offers a partial answer that describes the school context, not teacher characteristics: the extent to which at-risk students' needs differ from those of children who achieve academically; the congruity between the child's learning style and the characteristics of the program in which he or she is required to perform; the proportion of students whose learning styles diverge radically from the program's expectations. The report pinpoints only one characteristic of successful teachers, namely, the ability to personalize instruction under these conditions.[5]

In *White Teacher*, Vivian Paley describes her personal struggle to accept differences in her black students, observing that "anything a child feels is different about himself which cannot be referred to spontaneously, casually, naturally, and uncritically by the teacher can become a cause for anxiety and an obstacle for learning."[6] She argues that

> There is no activity useful only for the black child. There is no manner of speaking or unique approach or special environment required only for black children. . . . The challenge in teaching is to find a way of communicating to each child the idea that his or her special quality is understood, is valued, and can be talked about. It is not easy, because we are influenced by the fears and prejudices, apprehensions and expectations, which have become a carefully hidden part of every one of us.[7]

In their introduction to Paley's work, James Comer and Alvin Pouissant note that Paley taught in schools that were "well-supported, primarily middle class, and predominantly white."[8] They suggest that many more teachers like Paley, who understand, value, and discuss each child's special qualities, would emerge if they enjoyed the economic and administrative support that Paley could draw upon. Their contention is confirmed by a follow-up evaluation of former student teachers trained in a collaborative program between a university training center and an urban public school district. While student teachers successfully transferred, once they started teaching, many of the techniques they studied, saw demonstrated, and practiced in their training, several environmental factors inhibited or encouraged them in doing so: the availability of resources; the nature of administrative, staff and parental support; and their actual teaching assignment.[9]

What specifically are the conditions that make addressing student differences a Herculean task in urban schools? Unfortunately, as explained in the literature review, few writers have attempted to systematically apply to issues of teacher and student behavior, research about characteristics of urban school systems and schools. However, several studies, such as the report for the California State Department of Education noted above, confirm that the critical problem in urban teacher preparation is not to educate prospective teachers to deal with specific student characteristics but instead to assist them to interact with students of varying sensibilities and abilities in a setting that discourages this accommodation.

This conclusion is buttressed by another study conducted over 20 years ago in New York City. Four observers, all of them former New York City teachers, focused on how school procedures affected teachers' behavior.[10] They found seven recurring conditions in inner city junior high schools that undercut teachers' efforts to make their classes functioning groups.

1. A required adhesion to numerous school rules.
2. The seeming interchangeability of teachers and assignments.
3. The overspecialization of pedagogical functions.
4. An inordinate amount of class time spent on procedures designed to maintain school organization.
5. Little student or teacher control over assignments to classes.
6. Custodial treatment of children different in any way encouraged by the lock-step curriculum.
7. Much of the course content dictated by external examinations.[11]

These conditions combine to give an urban teacher no support and little opportunity to personalize instruction, as the California report warned successful teachers of at-risk students must do. In *The Preparation of Teachers, An Unstudied Problem in Education*, Seymour Sarason, Kenneth Davidson, and Burton Blatt conclude that individual differences of students complicate the teacher's task according to how much instruction enables children to act upon knowledge in ways that expand intellectual skills while reinforcing curiosity.[12] When this conclusion is combined with even the scanty research about urban school characteristics, the result indicates that a program of urban teacher preparations should assist prospective teachers to understand and resist conditions that rob learners and teachers of their individuality.

The problem of training teachers for urban schools is "not the same as preparing teachers to deal with racism in school and society" because teachers of poor, minority students do not need this understanding more—or less—than other teachers. *All* programs of teacher education should lead to an examination of one's own prejudices, in addition to understanding the problems and concerns of students and parents.[13] All teachers need to know how inequality is reflected in schooling.[14]

All teachers, as the NDEA Task Force noted, need to be able to deal with students as human beings, to be able to share knowledge and experience with students, to be trustworthy, to be able to communicate, and to understand their students' world. Urban teachers confront the greatest diversity of student needs, but the conditions in urban schools severely limit individualization, so the special demand made of urban teacher preparation is to educate teachers who can deal with students as individuals and human beings in settings that depersonalize learning, making students and teachers anonymous and powerless.[15]

The problem of preparing teachers of at-risk students in urban schools is then one of identifying how to educate teachers to allow ideals about teaching to prevail in a setting that undercuts these values and the teaching strategies that stem from them.

PREPARING TEACHERS FOR ETHNIC
AND RACIAL DIVERSITY

New urban teachers who are white or middle class will probably not teach students like themselves, as Carl Grant has observed, and they will work with students from a wide variety of cultures, both immigrant and native.[16] In fact, they will confront such a cultural potpourri that no program of teacher education can prepare them with information about all the cultures they may see in the course of even a relatively brief career in an urban school. Multicultural education, when presented as a body of sociological or historical data or a collection of unique instructional strategies, as it was in its fusion to competency-based teacher education (CBTE), is little help to an urban teacher who confronts a diverse, changing student population, as a study of the Teacher Trainee Program in Los Angeles suggests.[17] Learning about other cultures, as well as the deleterious effects of prejudice, and urging use of certain classroom techniques, as was done in the multicultural education training required for new teachers in the Los Angeles Unified School District (LAUSD), appeared to have little effect on participants' thinking.

The material presented in the LAUSD program, which is typical of preparation in multicultural relations that prospective teachers now receive, has roots in the scholarship of the 1970s, when educators and teacher educators accepted the vocabulary and premises of CBTE and used this pedagogy to teach prospective teachers about cultural differences. The premise of CBTE, that people can learn to teach well by mastering discrete skills and a body of knowledge, complements preparation in multicultural education that consists primarily of sociological data. However, if the aim of multicultural education is to help prospective teachers learn how to accommodate students' cultural differences in the classroom, with its dynamic and changing relations, then the content requires a different pedagogy, as I will discuss later in this chapter.

Indeed, multicultural education as it is usually taught is probably little help to any teacher, as research by the National Center for Research on Teacher Learning (NCRTL) indicates. In a large-scale study, NCRTL followed 700 teachers and teacher-candidates through their preparation program and into their first year of teaching. Despite coursework in multicultural education, teachers could not move beyond two contradictory moral imperatives: All children should be treated equally, and teachers should individualize to accommodate students' needs.[18]

Reconciling these two ideals is probably most difficult for urban teachers of at-risk students because individualization is so limited by bureaucratic strictures and yet students' needs are so diverse. Further, no urban teacher can be educated to be an expert about every ethnic group he or she will encounter in the schools today, and differences in culture are complicated by class and gender, and, for immigrants, other factors as well. For example, to speak of Hispanic culture masks the tremendous differences between Cuban and Puerto Rican immigrants, or between those immigrant families who have settled in this country and those who commute between their native country and a residence in the United States.[19] Teachers need the knowledge that culture, class, and gender influence how children learn and how families view education, but equally vital is the understanding that students who are demographically identical may be psychologically quite different, as, for instance, sisters and brothers frequently are. Teachers who are prepared to teach one kind of student, rather than learning how to learn from their teaching to adapt to individual differences, will find their preparation irrelevant.

My own experience in the New York City schools illustrates why it is futile to instruct prospective teachers about specific cultural traits students may bring to their learning, rather than assisting them to understand that differences of many sorts, some cultural, some personal, affect learning. To comply with funding allocations, New York City schools frequently transfer teachers involuntarily between schools, a policy called "excessing." Since excessing is done on the basis of seniority, teachers face the greatest number of transfers early in their careers.

Hence, the teachers with the least experience need the greatest skill in adapting to different student populations.

My first job in the New York City schools was in a high school that drew students from East Harlem (in Manhattan), a majority of them born in New York but native speakers of Spanish, many of them Puerto Rican. The school also contained a significant proportion of American blacks. Students were drawn from other boroughs, attending the school because of two magnet programs in the creative arts and nursing. At the end of my first year, I was transferred to Martin Luther King, about one mile away.

In my first three years King drew students from Harlem, as well as other boroughs, primarily American blacks who were native New Yorkers. The uniformity of their skin color belied the diversity of their backgrounds: Some were straight from small southern communities, still overwhelmed by living in New York and attending a school that was larger than their entire town; many others had strong family and religious ties, with working parents who monitored their activities closely; some were responsible for caring for their families, with parents who were drug addicts; others were drug dealers themselves.

In my fourth year at King, zoning changes for New York City high schools prompted significant shifts in the school's demographics. Some students from English-speaking islands in the Caribbean, the Virgin Islands and Grenada, for example, chose to attend King, which was safer than their local school in Brooklyn; students from South America excluded from an overcrowded neighboring high school came to King. In addition, Cambodian immigrants, previously enrolled in an English as a Second Language program within the school, began attending regular classes as their English improved. Thus, within two years I had significant numbers of students with expectations, problems, abilities, and needs different from those of the diverse population I already taught.

For the urban teacher, data about cultural differences, like other risk factors, are important in the same way that epidemiological evidence is valuable to a doctor. Epidemiology provides information that can narrow the range of diagnoses, but the information does not, by itself, dictate one particular diagnosis or treatment.[20] Just as doctors need to know how to apply epidemiological findings to clinical practice, to understand their usefulness and limitations, teachers need to understand how cultural, gender, and class differences pose risks to students and how using a range of teaching strategies can improve their chances of academic success.

One key to helping teacher-candidates to transcend stereotypes is to discuss how culture frames our development. One writer, comparing the starkly different views of black culture held by Richard Wright and Ralph Ellison, explained the disparity this way:

> Culture isn't something that comes with one's race or sex. It comes only through experience; there isn't any other way to acquire it. And in the end everyone's culture is different, because everyone's experience is different.[21]

While *all* teachers will be more effective if they know how to teach students of varying abilities and sensibilities, it is critical for the achievement of poor, minority students that their teachers have this capacity to reflect on and adapt their practice. When teaching occurs in urban classrooms, the need for preparation that develops this capability increases exponentially because school policies and structures discourage it.

A FRAMEWORK FOR THE SPECIAL PREPARATION OF URBAN TEACHERS

One of the few authors to focus on the problem of recruiting and preparing teachers specifically for urban schools in the past decade, Martin Haberman (1988), outlines several reforms for urban teacher preparation.

1. A major portion of university-based preparation should occur within the urban public school.
2. Courses should be taught by university faculty and master teachers from the school site.
3. New teacher education faculty should develop special urban education curricula.
4. New, functional partnerships are needed among parents, teachers, administrators, community members, and teacher preparation faculty.
5. A full-year internship should be required for certification in urban teaching.
6. States and school districts should provide resources for teacher preparation at school sites, redirecting state funds now given to schools of education.
7. Conditions of practice in urban schools should be improved.

Unlike most educators who have analyzed the problem of preparing teachers of at-risk students in urban schools, Haberman has taken into account the demands of the urban school context. However, his proposals do not take into account the dynamic interrelationship between the needs of students and conditions in urban schools. Like the alternative certification programs he criticizes, Haberman overemphasizes acquisition of special techniques and minimizes mastery of the reflective teaching that all teachers require, especially those who must mediate between students' needs and demands for instruction that seems useful and treatment that is personal, and the systemic requirements for uniform conduct and treatment.

The need for reflective teaching that integrates understanding of the social conditions of schooling demands a relationship between school and college different from the one that Haberman's proposals call for, as I explain later in this chapter.

In contrast to Haberman's focus on skill acquisition, Daniel Liston and Kenneth Zeichner observe in *Teacher Education and the Social Conditions of Schooling* that the aim of teacher preparation should be

> developing teachers who are able to identify and articulate their purposes, who can choose the appropriate instructional strategies or appropriate means, who know and understand the content to be taught, who understand the social experiences and cognitive orientations of their students, and who can be counted on for giving good reasons for their actions. These justifications should take into account the activity of teaching, the larger communities of educators, and a greater understanding of the social and political context of schooling.[22]

Urban teachers need this same preparation, and for the same reasons that Liston and Zeichner put forward to defend its usefulness in general. However, by stressing the deliberative and moral character of teaching and connecting it to the social and political context of schooling, Liston and Zeichner capture precisely the contradiction that makes teaching poor, minority children in urban schools so problematic. A moral imperative, the ideal of assisting students whose need for education is most critical to life success, must be maintained under school conditions that sabotage success and reduce teachers to "street-level bureaucrats." To work in these circumstances, teachers should understand what their own values and beliefs are, and how they have been shaped by social conditions, so that they can contend with institutional pressures to interact with students in ways that undermine their purposes.

Thus, while Liston and Zeichner do not discuss urban teacher preparation *per se*, their ideas are fully applicable, and in fact essential.

Only slight modifications need to be made for the segments of their text describing the aims of teacher education, teachers' knowledge, and the social context of schooling, for it to serve as an outline of what programs to prepare teachers of at-risk students in urban schools need to do and why.[23]

Liston and Zeichner explain that teacher preparation should encourage a reflective examination of prospective teachers' social beliefs and assumptions and our existing knowledge about the social conditions of schools. This framework assists teachers to justify their decisions with reference to their own values and the experiences that have shaped them, as well as to the social assumptions that underlie schooling and school organization. Liston and Zeichner insist that teacher candidates make reference to this context when articulating or justifying their decisions, so that they will confront issues of "empirical accuracy, moral persuasiveness, and political accuracy," which will assist them to "discern the respective value of distinct social or educational theories."[24]

This analysis acknowledges the need to take into account the class, gender, and race of teacher-candidates in their preparation. However, it only touches on the ways in which the program they outline has been influenced by their own students' educational and social backgrounds. Probably all of teacher preparation would benefit from examining this dimension more closely, but it is an essential component of urban teacher preparation because the social distance among urban teachers, their students, and the community tends to be far greater than it is in suburban schools. Therefore, one of the primary concerns of programs that educate prospective urban teachers should be to prepare them to bridge the chasm, caused by several factors. Urban schools are more isolated physically, in response to the violence that surrounds them, and they are more politically insulated, because of the massive bureaucracy that oversees their functioning. In addition, prospective teachers as a group tend to be young, white females who have grown up in small towns or rural areas and have no direct experience with public schools in cities or the students in them.[25]

Considering Race, Class, and Gender

Programs of teacher preparation have always been configured by race, class, and gender, although discourse about teacher preparation has seldom acknowledged or identified how these factors have combined to determine who receives what type of training. For example, elementary school teachers, overwhelmingly female, have been educated in normal schools and state teachers colleges; high school teachers, a majority of them male, have more likely received their training at universities.

Maurice Sedlak and Steven Schlossman explain that historically teachers have been drawn from three groups. Teachers from farms and rural areas provided the bulk of the teaching force until recently, when teachers from working class families born and raised in urban communities replaced the rural teachers. However, teaching has also attracted "high-status females" disproportionately because they "lacked a wide range of suitable alternatives and/or were committed to teaching as a missionary venture."[26] It is interesting to speculate about the extent to which recent debate about improving teacher quality masks quite another concern, recruiting more high-status candidates to teaching, and how this objective has influenced practices like usage of the National Teachers Exam to screen prospective teachers.

The concern about recruiting high-status teachers has not always been veiled. For instance, Harvard Graduate School of Education, from its inception, targeted an elite corps of applicants in devising its offerings. Similarly, in looking to recruit graduates from liberal arts colleges whose academic ability and leadership potential were above average for the profession, Master of Arts in Teaching (M.A.T.) programs in the 1960s recruited middle and upper middle class students, or in Sedlak and Schlossman's terms, high-status males and females drawn to teaching for idealistic reasons rather than as a means of moving out of the working class.[27]

Just as urban teachers should learn to identify and adapt to critical differences in students' needs, so must the programs that prepare them acknowledge and accommodate the marked differences among teacher candidates. Two pieces of scholarship are especially helpful in thinking through how the class backgrounds of teacher candidates should influence their preparation to teach in urban schools. One of them, by Peter Helmut Kelman, describes a rare attempt to shape teacher training to candidates' needs as well as to the demands of urban schools. Kelman conducted a needs assessment of the students enrolled in Wesleyan's Urban Master of Arts in Teaching program and concluded that the "teacher-scholar" orientation of most M.A.T. programs was not only irrelevant to the M.A.T. student's needs as an urban teacher, but was actually harmful. In reviewing the literature on difficulties of beginning and experienced urban teachers, he concluded that the "sociocultural approach" paid "scant attention to difficulties with the [school] administration or . . . the self."[28]

Many of the M.A.T. students' frustrations in the school setting resulted from their youth and idealism: They resented not being treated as professionals; they chafed at administrative directives and authoritarian supervisors; their ambitions and idealism made them unsympathetic to colleagues who seemed to share neither characteristic, and who were hostile that young newcomers were being trained to be educational leaders, that is, *their* leaders. Compounding these problems was the burden, for many, of meeting the adult responsibilities acquired in a first job.[29] Finally, their ambivalence about exercising authority made disciplining their classes a major problem, one that was not addressed by an M.A.T. program's heavy emphasis on scholarship and subject matter.

Gwyneth Dow reached the same conclusions as Kelman when she organized a new course of instruction for student teachers at the University of Melbourne. The student teachers, who resembled those in Wesleyan's Urban M.A.T. program, had great difficulty determining their identity as teachers because questions about who they were as adults fused with ideological concerns about establishing their classroom authority. "In trying to acquire a teaching style that fits them well, they have to face up to defining, living with and learning to act according to values that deeply satisfy them," Dow observed.[30]

Like Kelman, Dow argued against the teacher-scholar approach that the M.A.T. programs in universities generally favored. Instead, in her program students were taught how to ask questions about their subject areas since "even their whole concept of the subjects they had studied were quite often unsuited to school learning."[31] Furthermore, half the courses were offered at the school site, taught jointly by faculty of the school of education and teachers in the school, a strategy not unique to Dow's program or to training high-status teacher-candidates. However, Dow pinpointed a solution, which Kelman ignored, to the social and cultural conflicts the young, middle class, white M.A.T. students encountered: Closeness with one student was usually the key to a student teacher's unlocking some doubt or trouble. The greater the social and educational gulf between prospective urban teachers and the students they will teach, the greater the need to use Dow's insight in formulating programs of teacher preparation and, in particular, field experiences that should give teacher-candidates who are young, idealistic, and middle class opportunities to become close to individual students.

Early Field Experiences: The Perennial Panacea

Dow's and Kelman's work demonstrates that even widely accepted strategies in urban teacher preparation that seem to be universally effective, such as the importance of early field experience, need to be re-examined in light of teacher-candidates' characteristics. Differences among teacher-candidates may explain in part why research on field experiences in urban schools has been inconclusive. Different kinds of teacher-candidates need to have early field experiences adapted to their strengths and weaknesses within the urban school context, yet research on the usefulness of field experiences usually treats teacher-candidates as a homogeneous group, ignoring sociological, historical, and demographic data about who chooses teaching as a career.[32] The major exception to this occurred in the 1960s with educators who identified the cultural clash between teachers and disadvantaged students as causing low student achievement. However, their work dealt with student and teacher characteristics as static forces, ignoring the dynamic interrelationship between school conditions and teacher and student performance.

It may be, as the Association of Teacher Educators contends, that "research studies in teacher education consistently show that professional experiences [early field experiences, student teaching, practicums, and internships] are effective in shaping professional practice."[33] However, research does not explain how prospective teachers' attitudes and behaviors change, or why, let alone how characteristics of urban schools alter the scenario. Nor does it note how prospective teachers' values and experiences mitigate the effectiveness of a specific kind of field experience.

For example, three studies generated quite different conclusions about the benefits of field experiences. One, a dissertation comparing two undergraduate teacher training programs, concluded that following their preparation, students in the experimental program that provided increased early field experience showed a *less* positive attitude toward teaching than did students in the regular courses. A study of the effect of interning in schools serving disadvantaged students in urban schools found no differences in attitudes between these interns and a control group. The major indicators of all interns' attitudes, those teaching in the schools with disadvantaged students and those not, were their prior attitudes and the attitudes of their cooperating teachers. Still another study, using videotapes of teacher-candidates prior to and after student teaching, along with videos of cooperating teachers, showed that student teachers imitated only the techniques of their cooperating teachers that were effective.[34]

The greater the gulf between prospective teachers and their future students, the greater the need for prospective teachers to have field experiences that encourage them to become familiar and comfortable with individual students, so that students become real people rather than categories. When the early field experience encourages young, middle class teacher-candidates to assume teaching responsibilities or remain an observer, rather than establish relationships with individual students, the field experience subverts its most crucial objective.

Research I conducted with a group of Harvard student teachers similar to Kelman's group at Wesleyan confirms Dow's conclusion about why early field experiences are not necessarily helpful to all prospective urban teachers.[35] These young, idealistic student teachers struggled to reconcile their desire to change the world with their classroom practice. The conflict emerged primarily as a problem of exercising authority, determining who they were when they were in charge. Because they entered teaching to change education — and society — they had a considerable investment in making sure their classrooms were "democratic," or "free."

A young, female, middle class student teacher whom I supervised at Harvard needed such a field experience before student teaching in a Boston high school. Although she had no serious problems with classroom management and her teaching performance was outstanding, her student teaching was sufficiently stressful that she decided not to teach in an urban high school. Not until the very end of the term, she observed, did she become comfortable with the students, especially the boys. For most of the term she was secretly afraid of the students because, as she admitted, she had never known anyone who looked, talked, or acted like they did. Since she was particularly mature, confident in her mastery of the subject matter, and unambivalent about exercising her authority, her alienation did not prevent her from functioning well. However, she felt so estranged from most of the minority students that she did not enjoy her teaching as much as she had wanted to.

Again, my own early field experience provides an instructive case study. My social background was similar to that of teacher-candidates in M.A.T. programs, like the ones Kelman, Dunne, and Dow discuss, and like those I supervised at Harvard 20 years later. For my first field experience, I was sent to assist a teacher with a class of black teenagers, mostly girls, enrolled in a work-study program. Though I was 22, I had little experience working or socializing with teenagers, and even less familiarity with minority teens. They seemed hostile to me, but the teacher, a black woman several years older than I, had a friendly, relaxed relationship with them. Either she was unable to articulate how she achieved her easy manner of managing the class, or I did not know how to ask questions that would have helped me learn from her. To make the situation worse, the field experience never permitted me to get to know any of the students individually, for I was given responsibility for working with them as a group to produce a class newspaper.

Fortunately, my second field experience, student teaching in a racially and socially integrated urban high school, was excellent. My cooperating teacher turned over two of her classes immediately and gave me full responsibility for them. I was, however, very conscious about what I felt had been my inability to become familiar with and like my minority students in my first field experience. One incident illustrates just how anxious I was about learning to teach minority students. At the start of the term, I found distinguishing the faces of my Chinese students difficult, a problem I shared only with my closest friends because it embarrassed me. By October I had learned to recognize all of them, except for two boys (Andy and Homer), who shared the surname Wong with several other classmates. By November I despaired of ever telling the two apart and, ashamed, told no one.

After Thanksgiving vacation, I commented to Andy and Homer that they had both written in their journals about going to Los Angeles to visit an aunt. Andy gave me a puzzled, somewhat scornful look and said, "Of course! What do you think?"

Confused, I asked, "What do you mean?"

Homer, disgusted, replied, "We're brothers!"

"Brothers!"

"Yeah, twins! Didn't you know that! Don't you think we look the same?"

"Do your other teachers have trouble telling you apart?"

Andy answered that even his mother sometimes did.

Because my student teaching occurred in an integrated setting that contained some students who were familiar to me because they were white or middle class, I felt less alienated than I had in the first field experience. I gained enough confidence as a teacher to work through many of my fears about teaching poor, minority students, as the incident with the Wong twins illustrates. Yet, despite the overwhelmingly positive experience of student teaching, that first field experience with minority students was so stressful that, like the student teacher I supervised many years later, I decided not to teach in an urban school when I completed my training.

Not all white, middle class teacher-candidates feel alienated from students in urban schools. Those who feel comfortable with youngsters in the age group they will teach, such as those who are older parents or those who want to teach elementary school and have a great deal of experience with young children, may have little trouble establishing a relationship with students who are not from a similar social background. The early field experience probably should serve a different purpose for them, as it should for many prospective teachers who come from working class backgrounds.

The literature on teacher preparation contains little by or about working class students who aspire to teach, yet these are the students who provide the bulk of the teaching force. Young, white, female prospective teachers who are products of urban school systems or the lower tracks in public schools present another set of requirements for field experiences to be successful, as my work at Jersey City State College has shown me.

Most of the students in our undergraduate teacher preparation program are young women who come from lower middle or working class families. Many of the white students come from Catholic ethnic groups and have attended urban parochial schools from kindergarten through high school. Those students from minority groups share very much the same educational experiences as the pupils they will teach. Most of the female students who want to become elementary school teachers have already had considerable experience working with young children, and their ambivalence about asserting authority is not linked to an analytical appraisal of the relationship among classroom practice, educational reform, and social change, at least not to the degree that it was for my Harvard students.

For students who have never been exposed to the teaching practices that are most frequently found in the high academic tracks, the early field experience is a precious opportunity to observe classrooms of urban teachers who withstand institutional pressures for uniform instruction and custodial treatment of students. The field experience must persuade many teacher-candidates that, contrary to what they have personally experienced as learners, the strategies and techniques that are modeled and taught in their preparation to teach can be used successfully in urban schools.

Teacher-candidates who view teaching as a career, as working class students are more likely to do than their high-status counterparts, are more susceptible to institutional pressures to conform, for many reasons. Unlike their middle class counterparts, many of whom view teaching as a way station between undergraduate school and the career they will pursue, young, white, working class women are frequently the first members of their families to attend college. Teaching is their foothold out of the working class, and their student teaching introduces them to the milieu in which they will root themselves. Further, these young working class women, unlike their older counterparts who have worked in other jobs or raised families, are less likely to have been exposed to life experiences that demand that they make crucial life choices. For the most part, they have never lived on their own because for financial reasons they remain at home while they attend college and do their student teaching. Finally, their motivations for choosing teaching as a career are not generally connected to an articulated perspective about teaching's relationship to social change, as were the motivations of teacher-candidates at Harvard, for instance. With the exception of the young black and Hispanic women, few of the working class students express a desire to use teaching to improve social conditions.

These young women frequently lack the intellectual tools to reflect critically on educational practice. Thus their early field experience should be linked to coursework that stresses developing their ability to reflect critically about their teaching. This, in turn, depends on their having an understanding of educational theory and the subject matter they will teach.

Fusing Educational Theory and Subject Matter Knowledge

In their outline for reforming teacher education, Liston and Zeichner address the prospective teacher's need to know and understand the content to be taught and to choose appropriate teaching strategies. While all teachers will be better for having these abilities, teaching well in an urban setting demands them: Urban teachers must know how to create breathing space in an environment that is intellectually suffocating because of scarce resources and curricular mandates. Urban teachers must devise lessons that prepare students to succeed on all manner of tests that call for mastery of decontextualized pieces of information, while simultaneously creating an intellectually stimulating climate that seduces students to attend class and resist the pull of the streets. One experienced social studies teacher recounted an experience that captured the dilemma. She had participated in the state-wide committee selecting the pool of questions to be used for the competency test in social studies. The questions were, she observed, "fair" but "antiseptic" and "sterile." The next term she taught a remedial class to coach seniors who had failed the test and needed to pass in order to graduate. They were "slow," she noted, in mastering the test questions but insightful when discussing racial and ethnic divisions in American society, in particular a recent conflict between Koreans and blacks in a Brooklyn neighborhood. At first the students decided racial tensions were inevitable, but when given the assignment to generate a list of measures to defuse the confrontation that had occurred, the class produced a plan that was identical to the compromise devised weeks later by representatives of city government. Their work was greatly facilitated by the contribution of two students, one Cambodian, the other Thai, who described cultural norms and behaviors that were frequently misinterpreted by Americans.[36]

The teacher noted, proudly, how the students demonstrated the cognitive and affective skills needed to assess and mediate racial conflicts; but she ruefully acknowledged that the competency test in American government would probably not measure mastery of these abilities or the specific knowledge that had been learned about Korean and Thai culture. Still, she hoped that this highly successful project would nurture the students' interest in government and motivate them to master information about topics she had no time to develop fully but anticipated might be tested and would therefore present in summary fashion.

Urban teachers, like most others, do not receive preparation that harnesses a mastery of educational theory to subject matter knowledge. This is not a new problem; historically in preparing urban teachers, indeed the mass of teachers, subject matter knowledge and mastery of educational theory have been separated from and subordinated to acquisition of teaching skills. These two domains, the practical and the theoretical, parallel a persistent dichotomy in programs of teacher preparation, a distinct division of labor in teacher training: one to train the mass of teachers; the other, educational leaders.

It is instructive to note that early in his career, John Dewey defended this dichotomy. He argued that the first tier of teachers would master technique while a much smaller group would focus on "pedagogical discussion and experimentation." However, between 1894 and 1904 Dewey's thinking about teacher preparation changed dramatically, and by the end of his time at the University of Chicago he was convinced that educational experimentation and teacher education had an organic interdependence and were the Siamese twins of educational improvement.[37]

Dewey's initial distinction between training the mass of teachers and an elite who would be leaders, one he subsequently rejected as politically and pedagogically unsound, has characterized teacher preparation for the past century. In an essay, "The Relation of Theory to Practice in Education," Dewey explained why the prospective teacher cannot learn how to apply educational theory to subject matter when preparation to teach stresses mastery of "practical" skills. Identifying this as the "apprenticeship" model, Dewey explained how it made the teacher technically adept, at the cost of acquiring habits of observation, insight, and reflection that make the student of education a thoughtful and alert teacher who can extrapolate from analysis of his or her own learning to understand how others may learn. Further, Dewey warned, it encourages intellectual dependence that allows teachers to be led, sheep-like, from one "education gospel" to another, and to become submerged in rules, regulations, reports, and percentages, especially when they become administrators. The education student must learn to observe classes from a psychological standpoint to become an individual judge and critic of practical devices used by other teachers and to avoid mere imitation, Dewey concluded.[38]

Dewey argued that all teachers need an ability to "carry back subject-matter to its common psychical roots." A mind that is

> habituated to viewing subject matter from the standpoint of the function of that subject matter in connection with mental responses, attitudes, and methods will be sensitive to signs of intellectual activity . . . [and able to] call out and direct mental activity . . . [based on] a spontaneous and unconscious appreciation of the subject matter.[39]

Dewey explained that after prospective teachers

> appropriate new subject matter (thereby improving their own scholarship and realizing more consciously the nature of the method), they should finally proceed to organize this same subject-matter with reference to its use in teaching others.[40]

Lawrence Cremin suggested a similar formulation about subject matter preparation in *The Education of the Educating Professions*. In addition to having had the experience of thinking "seriously about the substance of a liberal education . . . about the relationships among the several fields of knowledge," the prospective teacher

> should ideally have mastered some field of knowledge of art sufficiently well to have been able to reflect systematically on the various ways in which it might be taught to clients at different stages of development and in different teaching situations.[41]

Using Dewey's terms then, to be effective, *all* teachers should have the ability to understand the "psychical roots" of their subject matter, the questions that underlie their disciplines. However, this is most essential for teachers of students who neither automatically accept the cultural assumptions of traditional curricula, nor see much reason to believe that mastery of the material will be useful to them, as is the case with teachers of poor, minority students in urban schools.

Put another way, if students can succeed in school without true intellectual engagement with the substance of instruction, and their teachers do not provide it, the students are cheated of one of schooling's dearest functions, but they will still succeed academically because, unfortunately, intellectual engagement is not essential for success in school.[42] When students need to connect with a discipline's psychical roots to master material, and the teacher is not able to reflect on how the subject matter can best be presented so that students can engage with it, then he or she cheats the students of both intellectual engagement and the opportunity for school success. Finally, the urban teacher of at-risk students must attempt to compensate in his or her classroom for the system's curricular mandates, combating the "aggregate picture of school learning," which is "fragmented" and "superficial."[43]

Insofar as ability tracking has dominated schooling, teacher candidates are products of these tracks. As Gwyneth Dow observed, superior academic achievement does not guarantee the kind of mastery of subject matter that is necessary for effective teaching; however, teacher-candidates who are graduates of high tracks and elite undergraduate colleges are more likely to have been exposed to instructional techniques that encouraged them to reflect on subject matter.

On the other hand, teacher-candidates drawn from poor and working class families are less likely to have been exposed to learning situations in which their opinions and ideas have been valued.[44] One of the most critical objectives of a program preparing these students to teach in urban schools with at-risk students must be to expose them to alternative models of teaching and learning. While all their coursework in education should, of course, be pedagogically exemplary, methods courses provide a unique opportunity for them to experience *as students* the same instructional techniques and strategies they can employ as teachers. Helping them to understand how they learn best, and why, is one key to motivating them to acquire the teaching skills they need to prevail against systemic constraints.

My experience teaching on the Staten Island campus of the City University of New York confirmed for me why the examination of prospective teachers' own learning should be emphasized in preparing working class students to teach in urban schools. In the course on methods of teaching English in secondary schools, all students were obligated to observe English classes in local high schools. All were undergraduates, residents of Staten Island, and white. The objective of the course, as I explained to them in our first session, was to assist them to acquire a personal philosophy of teaching English and an understanding of the techniques that would help them to carry out their philosophy in an urban high school, where most intended to teach. Since the dominant mode of instruction in city schools was a teacher-centered approach, primarily using lecture and a 40-minute, self-contained lesson, I explained I would model another type of instruction, a student-centered approach, identified in our textbook as the open-classroom model.

As several students commented in their final examination, they were puzzled, confused, and frustrated for much of the course because I refused to lecture about how to teach English. Instead, our coursework paralleled the kinds of activities that characterize a student-centered language arts classroom: small group activities; open-ended whole class discussions; brainstorming; double-entry notebooks; free-writing; panels; active listening. When we discussed a specific technique, for example, correcting students' use of nonstandard English, I would ask the students to identify advantages and disadvantages, as well as the values implicit in the decision to use the technique.

What was most surprising for me was their reluctance to present their own opinions. When I assigned them the task of responding to a reading by describing a personal reaction, *any* reaction, all but two students handed in pure summaries. In class, we discussed the reasons they had interpreted the assignment as they had. We examined how I had presented the assignment, and I explained that in giving them instructions I had not stressed the importance of explaining their reactions, because in my experience as a high school teacher, students were more likely to err by describing their responses fully while ignoring all references to the text. They had done the opposite. "Why?" I asked.

Unknowingly, they repeated arguments about cultural reproduction in schooling. To succeed in school they had accepted that their opinions were not as valuable as those of the "experts," and the teacher was an expert. They had never questioned this premise, nor had their instructors. During the field experience component of the course, they noticed that students in honors classes were frequently asked their opinions and encouraged to question material they read, whereas students in remedial classes were expected to absorb information. Their own experiences in school had, for the most part, been somewhere in between these two extremes, and most were deeply affected by the contrast.

Their intellectual self-confidence limited their ability to question traditional teaching methods. One student made this connection explicit, starting with an explanation about why, after much thought, he had decided that he was opposed to ability groupings.

It seems like a common sense idea, take all the smart kids, put them together, and they will learn faster. The less fortunate ones, the slow ones, when placed in the same class can learn at a slower pace. What this does is send out disturbing signals to children. The slow ones may become bored by the slow pace of teaching they receive. Classes set up for slow students often use unimaginative reading materials when these are the students who are most in need of having imagination stirred. It is disturbing for students to realize at such an early age that they have been stigmatized with the label "slow," and it can easily turn into a self-fulfilling prophesy. This also discounts the value that so-called "slow" students can bring to a classroom. Reading levels measure one facet of a child; it doesn't measure artistic ability, story telling, or necessarily intelligence.

I was taught all through school that one person's opinion counted, the instructor's. This is ingrained in me and I found it hard to rebel against this notion throughout the term. What my fellow students wrote on my papers didn't concern me, they weren't grading me, and I didn't learn that way. I think that's wrong. I don't act that way outside of the classroom so I shouldn't in . . . so now I think that students in English should learn how to *learn* from their peers. I think each of us does it instinctively outside of a classroom setting, and it is only when we sit in a desk and listen to an instructor lecture that we forget about the teacher sitting beside us.[45]

Another student commented:

I have finally realized why school has never been much fun. I was treated like a machine. I was the can recycler. Knowledge was put into me like the can is put into the machine; I then spit out the information condensed just as the can is spit out of the machine condensed. Do you think I was having any fun? Well, neither was I. Because of this my report cards consistently read "N. is very bright, but she is not working to her potential." That is because I was trained to work to their potential.[46]

How should methods courses address the sharp differences in values that underlie a teacher's decision to employ one instructional technique rather than another, for instance, to stress competition rather than collaboration? Here again, the social background of teacher-candidates is an essential consideration. White, middle class students who choose to teach in urban schools, as Kelman and Dunne explain, are frequently motivated by political idealism. For many of them, urban teaching is a political act, and before enrolling in their program of preparation, they are already familiar with and convinced by arguments that schools reproduce social and economic inequality, when instead they should be cultivating a cultural pluralism. Working class students are less likely to arrive at a teacher preparation program with these political convictions and motivations to teach.[47]

Although I explain in Chapter 5 why I reject arguments that prospective teachers must accept an emancipatory political ideology, some further comments are relevant here. As I have observed in teaching working class students, it is very possible, even likely, for prospective teachers to have a pedagogical philosophy that teachers must assist all students to fulfill their potential and to also have conservative political opinions, for example, that all ethnic groups should assimilate. To teach well, educators need not have uniform political beliefs about the extent to which minority group members are oppressed or should assimilate, or about schooling's role as a vehicle for social reform; but they do need to acknowledge that the social context of schooling affects teachers and students and to understand how conditions in urban schools make academic success more difficult for poor, minority students.

Teacher educators can rightfully insist that all prospective teachers have at their fingertips a range of instructional technique and strategies that assist students to succeed. However, teacher educators should not demand uniform thinking about how and when these strategies should be employed. Indeed, a glaring irony of the strategy to make teachers agents of social change and political liberation is that while it purports to use teacher education to emancipate poor and working class students, it contains a bias toward middle class teacher-candidates by insisting that effective teachers agree with a world view more frequently held by liberal, middle class graduates of elite colleges than by the working class graduates of public colleges.

To the extent that prospective teachers to not know how to return to the psychical roots of the subjects they teach, they are incapable of transcending curricular requirements. Even when their coursework in teacher preparation models this type of pedagogy, it cannot by itself compensate for their previous experiences in kindergarten through high school and college. This is another reason that the involvement of liberal arts faculty in teacher preparation is essential, which Trainers of Teacher Trainers demanded as part of parity.

One of the most serious errors in designs for professional development schools has been the absence of institutional involvement by liberal arts faculty. While this is an important flaw if the professional development school prepares teacher-candidates who were in high academic tracks or graduated from elite liberal arts programs, it is considerably more so if the prospective teachers have no personal educational experience to use to compare the kind of learning they have had with the kind of teaching they should do.

USING THE URBAN SETTING

Tension between theory and practice heightens as teacher candidates' intended work settings contrast more dramatically with the college or university ambience in which they are trained. Like all good teachers, urban teachers of poor, minority students need to master a wide range of teaching strategies, but they require another ability as well — using these techniques in a setting that discourages experimentation.[48] To resist institutional pressures for custodial treatment of children who fare poorly with the standardized instruction urban school systems rely on so heavily, urban teachers must have a developed understanding of how children learn. But they must also acquire the skills that will produce a classroom environment that permits them to learn about student differences. All of these goals are accomplished most successfully when prospective teachers have field experiences in urban schools, reinforced by coursework addressing the urban school context and conditions within it.

I have explained why the specific characteristics of programs that prepare urban teachers should depend in great part on the teacher-candidates enrolled, but first-hand experience and theoretical knowledge about urban schools are essential for virtually all prospective teachers who will work with poor, minority students in urban schools. In general, the less familiar the candidates are with an urban school setting and the students in it, the more experience they need working with students in that context. This explains why, as Larry Cuban has argued, an effective teaching model for inner city students also applies to suburban schools, but not vice versa.[49] Teachers who learn to respect students' differences and teach them as individuals under bureaucratic conditions have little problem adjusting to a less pressured context. Similarly, experienced suburban teachers who have internalized the process of reflective teaching can probably adjust to urban schools that discourage its use, if they choose to teach in urban schools with less favorable working conditions.

To some extent, geography has exacerbated the problem of providing prospective urban teachers with practical experience. In most states, teacher education occurs on college campuses located in small towns where teachers complete their practice teaching, so they have no experience teaching in urban school conditions.[50] The first step in correcting this problem is to understand that field experiences in programs preparing teachers for urban elementary and secondary schools should occur in regular urban schools, so that prospective teachers learn first-hand how to cope with the special circumstances they will confront in urban classrooms.

As the NDEA Task Force report suggested, working conditions and student behavior are indeed reasons teachers in "deprived areas" fail, but understanding their symbiosis is essential for assisting urban teachers to manage their classrooms well. Thus their training should direct prospective teachers to examine the social conditions and school characteristics that encourage students to behave as they do, but teacher-candidates must also learn the techniques that successful urban teachers use to reconcile the legitimate demands of students and the constraints imposed on them.

Although urban school conditions create special problems in classroom management, the difference between the elementary and high school setting has not been the subject of much research in preparing urban teachers of poor, minority students.[51] For example, urban high school teachers contend with five times as many students in schools, which are themselves four or five times larger than urban elementary schools, so an anonymity prevails that makes establishing relationships with students—and a student teacher's own cooperating teacher—far more difficult. Furthermore, high school teachers are much closer in age to their students, a situation that can also make classroom management more problematic. Because teaching is departmentalized and broken down into 40-minute blocks, high school teachers have less flexibility. In addition, the subject matter they teach exerts its own demands, regardless of how the departments are arranged.[52]

These considerations hold for high school teaching generally, not just that in urban schools or with at-risk students. However, they are more critical factors in urban teacher preparation because they are exacerbated by conditions in urban schools. For example, though suburban and urban high schools may both be large and anonymous, students and teachers in wealthier suburban schools are more likely to have access to counselors' assistance because the schools are better funded and have lower student to counselor ratios.[53] Teachers in suburban high schools, like their urban cohorts, will have difficulty finding time in school to call parents of the 150 or so students they teach; but the suburban teachers will have ready access to a phone in school, a luxury many urban teachers can only dream about.

Many urban school systems use competitive exams to track students into elite, vocational, and comprehensive high schools, and new high school teachers will most likely teach in the most difficult conditions, in a comprehensive high school with remedial classes. These schools have the highest concentrations of students with academic and social needs ignored by the urban school systems and they generally offer the least support to faculty.[54] Therefore, the teacher's mastery of classroom management skills is of the utmost urgency. Teachers in urban comprehensive high schools have little room for error in establishing their authority and a climate of mutual respect, and student teaching must give new teachers who will work in these schools the confidence and practice they need to organize instruction and relate to students.

Another contrast between student teaching in urban elementary and high schools is in the relationship between the intern and cooperating teacher. Because the elementary classroom is self-contained and the school itself a less anonymous environment, the intern in a grade school is likely to have a more intense relationship with the cooperating teacher. While this generates a duel for control of the class, it also makes for closer supervision and more opportunity for feedback.

Programs that prepare teachers for urban schools need to find methods of compensating for the anonymity with which interns, like the urban students they instruct and the cooperating teachers with whom they work, must contend. One popular solution is to group interns in school sites and conduct some portion of their college training in the school, so that they feel less isolated. My research indicates that another key is to ensure that interns have frequent contact with their college supervisors.[55]

Classroom management is a major concern for most new or soon-to-be teachers, but the issue has an urgency for urban teachers that should be reflected in their preparation, especially if they are likely to have ideological doubts about exerting their authority. Carl Grant recommends that urban teacher preparation include teaching an entire class of urban students for at least several months under the guidance of a senior teacher who knows how to teach urban students.[56] I would refine his suggestion to have student teaching commence the first day of the school term and conclude with the end of the semester, so that the student teacher assumes responsibility for establishing classroom regulations and enforcing them from start to finish. The widely accepted practice of introducing student teachers gradually to their responsibilities—having them start with one class or time slot, and adding more teaching time as the semester progresses, so that the intern teaches a full five-period load for a few weeks at the end of the college's academic term—is counterproductive. It robs urban student teachers of the chance to experience the consequences of erring in establishing class procedures and working through the problem with assistance from a college supervisor and cooperating teacher. Further, it makes donning the mantle of authority more problematic for all parties—students, cooperating teacher, and student teacher—by blurring the answer to the question "Who's in charge here?" Finally, when the teacher-candidate becomes a regular teacher, working full-time, mistakes can create problems that are overwhelming, and in the most difficult urban high schools assistance is usually impossible to obtain.

Having urban student teachers assume total responsibility for a limited number of courses or, at the elementary level, for part of the day, for an entire school term or semester is one method of giving prospective teachers the confidence and understanding they need, but there are other methods of organizing student teaching to accomplish this same purpose, which I do not mean to exclude by describing this particular solution at length. What is most important is using the urban setting to give student teaching the three characteristics that Dewey argued, correctly I think, specially designed lab or practice schools cannot: intellectual responsibility; responsibility for classroom management; responsibility to the occupation rather than to a supervisor.

DIFFERENTIATING ROLES AND RESPONSIBILITIES IN PREPARING URBAN TEACHERS

Nathan Glazer contends that in the schools of the minor professions like education and social work, tension between the ideals of the academy and the professions as they are practiced is eradicable. His work suggests that Martin Haberman's argument for differentiated roles for schools of education and schools in urban teacher preparation is correct, and that neither alone can provide optimal preparation. However, defining these differentiated roles depends first on clarifying the relationship between theoretical training and practical work, then deciding how the roles should be divided.[57]

This topic is by itself the subject for a comprehensive study, but in brief I think most coursework in teacher preparation is by its nature theoretical and therefore should be taught by instructors who are given time and resources to remain in touch with developments and debates in research. Ideally, all public school teachers would have reduced teaching responsibilities, so that they would have the time and opportunity to examine their practice in light of current research, but as long as the work lives of college instructors and classroom teachers differ so dramatically, coursework in teacher preparation should be conducted by college personnel, who are correctly expected to be knowledgeable about research even if they do not conduct it themselves.

For this reason, I think one currently popular proposal of linking school and college, having classroom teachers conduct methods courses in conjunction with college faculty, gives the classroom teacher a responsibility that can be fulfilled only if the classroom teacher is exploited. Even when classroom teachers in city schools have half a regular teaching load, their responsibilities resemble the full-time teaching load of college faculty. It is unreasonable to expect classroom teachers to shoulder even part of their commitment to a public school while teaching a methods course and remaining knowledgeable about current research.

In the conflict between theory and practice that the college and the school site represent, teacher preparation belongs more in the domain of theory and the purview of the college. As many public school teachers acknowledge when they return to college for additional coursework, the ivory tower does isolate its inhabitants, but it can give them a perspective that is restorative in its idealism. Prospective teachers, especially those who will work with poor, minority students under conditions that reinforce failure, need to have the "ideal," which they see little of in urban schools, emphasized in their preparation, to gird them against the "real," which they see and hear far too much of when they teach.

On the other hand, the college faculty need to keep in touch with school reality. One important outcome of making educational research attend to local knowledge is that when public school teachers, students, and community members help frame researchers' questions and answers, they contribute to the usefulness of content in teacher preparation programs. For example, when teacher educators use Michelle Fine's or John Ogbu's research, which gives voice to the otherwise silenced voices of students, prospective teachers are assisted in understanding why urban students drop out of school and why urban teachers don't seem to be able to stop them.

The link between college and school is the college supervisor of field experiences. Ironically, the proposals for teacher reform that have emanated from major research universities, like the Holmes Group, over the past decade have failed to address the common practice of subcontracting the labor-intensive job of supervision to graduate students, who are in turn supervised by a faculty member. While research literature identifies field experiences as being the most critical element in any program of teacher preparation, it is the one least likely in research universities to have the immediate involvement of full-time faculty.

In urban teacher preparation this practice is unsupportable, for detailed knowledge of specific school sites and the ability to bring the authority of the college to bear on problems are essential.[58] When interns are placed in urban schools, their situation must be closely monitored, because they are subject to more intense pressures to conform to standardized procedures, and because they are vulnerable to far more abuses than they are in school systems that have fewer crises with which to grapple. If a school principal directs interns to do clerical work in the office because information on student transfers is not being processed to teachers fast enough, or if an assistant superintendent assigns an intern with a Spanish surname to work in a bilingual class because the teacher will be going on maternity leave in a few weeks and he needs someone to cover the class—two situations I have intervened to change—the college supervisor should have the authority and expertise to correct the problem. Moreover, college supervisors are key to identifying and recruiting exemplary cooperating teachers, as well as pressuring college and school site administrators who arrange field experience placements to use these teachers. Even the most talented and knowledgeable graduate students and adjunct faculty are unlikely to be able to perform these functions because they lack longevity in the job and access to internal decision making.

Cooperating teachers who assist in preparing urban teachers reinforce and model "teaching against the grain," withstanding pressures to conform to school policies and norms they believe are detrimental to students.[59] This is especially vital when prospective teachers will work with at-risk students who are frequently blamed for their lack of academic success. In addition, cooperating teachers provide a wealth of first-hand knowledge about how to deal with the urban school bureaucracy, how to find scarce resources, and which regulations and procedures can be circumvented. These sound like low level skills, but they often make the difference between an exhausting but tolerable first year of urban teaching and one that is simultaneously a disastrous introduction and conclusion to urban teaching.

Two major concerns should distinguish a program that prepares teachers who will educate poor, minority children in urban school systems. First, the focus should be to equip candidates to mediate between the inflexibility of school procedures and practices on the one hand, and the diverse needs of students and teachers on the other. Second, the preparation must accommodate differences among teacher-candidates so that they learn how to deal with students who differ from each other and the teacher.

When programs to prepare urban teachers of at-risk students are not socially and racially heterogeneous, fulfilling these two objectives becomes far more problematic. Segregated urban schooling has been an unacknowledged and immutable given in most scholarship on urban education and policy making for the past decade, and so have segregated programs of teacher preparation, as the pool of prospective minority teachers has shrunken. Courses that explore the social context of urban schooling are incomparably enriched by participation of students who can share their first-hand experience about, for example, what occurs in *all* the tracks, remedial as well as honors. Although most of the concern about recruitment of minority teachers has focused on the need for them to serve as role models, little has been written about the deleterious consequences of having minority students absent from programs of teacher preparation.

TEACHING AT-RISK STUDENTS IN URBAN SCHOOLS: A CALLING AND A JOB

While all teachers face the dilemma of dealing with students' individual differences within an institutional setting, those who have the largest number of students, as well as the greatest percentage in circumstances that require individual attention, and the fewest resources to satisfy individuals, confront the tension in its most concentrated form. Students and parents who are habitually denied the special attention they require are likely to become more easily frustrated when they are once again put off. Thus, urban teachers of at-risk students face harder choices more frequently because of the juxtaposition of consistently scarce resources, continually pressing need, and institutional pressures to ignore the conflict.

The capacity to retain one's ideals while functioning in a setting that undercuts them is an ability no program of teacher preparation can ensure. In fact, this tension is probably what makes Haberman correct when he argues that a lifetime of urban teaching is an unrealistic goal.[60] The central problem in teaching at-risk students in urban schools is the friction between urban teaching's demands as a calling, that is, the moral and political value of providing at-risk students with the education they urgently need, and its restrictions as a job, the systemic limitations the teacher confronts daily to fulfill the calling. As James Comer explains, this tension explains why so many teachers seem not to care about their students' success: In accommodating to the job's restrictions, they subordinate their ideal of teaching as a calling. Without understanding this conflict, prospective urban teachers of at-risk students will be ill-equipped to survive with ideals intact.

Aside from meeting the requirements that apply to quality programs to educate teachers, the preparation of teachers of at-risk students in urban schools needs to take into account the social context of urban schooling and the characteristics of prospective teachers. What is critical in formulating programs to prepare teachers of at-risk students in urban schools is matching the program to the teacher-candidates' abilities and values so that they enter urban schools prepared to teach students with an unlimited variety of needs, many of them beyond schooling's purview, under pressures for both teacher and student to conform to standardized procedures.

This study was originally motivated by my desire to learn why, as a successful teacher of at-risk students, I found myself struggling during my first year at an urban high school. I believe I have explained my own experience, as well as the trajectory of many other teachers who leave urban schools after disheartening, short-lived careers. Prospective teachers can be equipped with the knowledge, confidence, and skills to teach successfully in urban schools, but only if programs that prepare them eschew the effort to identify discrete characteristics that make good teachers of at-risk students and focus instead on how the demands of the urban school setting subvert school success for poor, minority students and job satisfaction for their teachers.

One of the most painful experiences for urban teachers is to hear students, parents, administrators, or citizens complain that teachers don't care. The same, of course, is true for students, parents, and administrators, who are also called uncaring when they fail to meet others' expectations for behavior and attitude. Usually the problem is that school conditions have made communication among the parties extraordinarily difficult. One classic example is what occurs when students miss a great deal of school. Frequently, urban teachers experience the long-term absentee's return to school as a futile gesture, and indeed, as the statistics indicate, school absence is closely correlated with dropping out. However, for the student, the return to school is frequently an expression of hope, or at least ambivalence. The teacher, beset by responsibilities for the students who have been attending more regularly, may do nothing more than remind the returning student that he or she must make up missed work. With this, teachers satisfy their official responsibilities, although the student's presence is a reminder that their moral responsibilities have not been met. The student, accustomed to this kind of treatment, records it as another example of the conditions that make success in school impossible and attendance useless.

Neither party has been fulfilled in this interaction; neither has been able to succeed. This destructive symbiosis can be eliminated only by insisting that school reform begin from the premise that all parties benefit from a school environment that minimally allows, and optimally nurtures, communication and cooperation among education's constituencies.

Notes

Introduction

1. These ideas are described more fully in the preface to Lipow's 1983 study, *Authoritarian Socialism in America: Edward Bellamy and the Nationalist Movement.* Much of my political thinking corresponds to the ideas explained in Draper's *The Two Souls of Socialism.*

2. Manny, 1915, p. 63.

3. Ibid. The report does not specify whether classes for "foreign pupils" were for students who were foreign-born, the children of immigrants, or both.

4. Ibid., p. 94.

5. Ibid., p. 96.

6. Cuban, 1987, p. 349.

7. Carnegie Forum, 1986, executive summary, n.p.

8. Sykes, 1986, p. 365.

9. Edelfelt, Corwin, and Hanna, 1974, p. 12.

10. Cuban, 1987, pp. 351, 352.

11. Comer, 1975; Davies, 1987.

12. Comer, 1975, p. 162.

13. Davies, 1987.

14. Liston and Zeichner, 1990.

15. Leslie, Levin, and Wampler, 1971.

Chapter 1

1. Storen, 1964, p. 24.

2. Ibid., p. 25.

3. Ibid., p. 1.

4. Hunt, 1969, p. vii.

5. Downing et al., 1965.

6. Riessman, 1962, p. 3.

7. Ibid., p. 82.

8. Comer, 1975, p. 166.

9. Adams, Ahmad, and Jameson, 1969, p. 359.

10. Adams, Sobin, and Lockerman, 1969, preface.

11. Passow, Goldberg, and Tannenbaum, 1967, introduction.

12. Leacock, 1971, p. 9.

13. Webster's New Collegiate Dictionary, 2nd. ed., s.v. "disadvantaged" and "deprived."

14. Goldberg, 1967, p. 50.

15. Deutsch, 1967, p. 217.
16. Dodson, 1967.
17. Eisenberg, 1967, Editors' preface, p. 78.
18. Castro, 1971; Drucker, 1971.
19. Goodman, 1966.
20. Larner, 1966, p. 11.
21. Parker, 1968, p. 32.
22. O'Brian, 1969, p. 172.
23. Larner, 1966, p. 25.
24. Goodman, 1966, p. 67.
25. Adelman, 1970, p. 74.
26. Furno and Kidd, 1974, preface.
27. Ibid., p. vi.
28. Ibid., p. 138.
29. Dunne, 1973.
30. Parker, 1968, p. 32.
31. Hite and Drummond, 1975, p. 133.
32. Bell, 1975, p. 99.
33. Cuban, 1970.
34. Washington, D.C. Public Schools, 1968.
35. Bell, 1975.
36. Cuban, 1970, p. 150.
37. Hite and Drummond, 1975, p. 133.
38. Dunne, 1973; Parker, 1968; Steffensen, 1975; Washington, 1964; Washington, D.C. Public Schools, 1968.
39. Parker, 1968, p. 96.
40. Kreuter, 1966.
41. Ibid.
42. Berube, 1966, p. 72.
43. O'Brian, 1969, p. 167.
44. Ibid., p. 169.
45. Downing et al., 1965.
46. Smith et al., 1969.
47. Ibid., p. ix.
48. Ibid., p. 4.
49. Ibid., p. 13.
50. Ibid., p. 11.
51. Downing et al., 1965, p. 189.
52. Smith et al., 1969, p. 27.
53. Ibid., p. 70.
54. Ibid., p. 71.
55. Ibid., p. 5.
56. Cuban, 1970, p. xx.
57. Ibid., p. 21.
58. Steffensen, 1975.
59. Cuban, 1970, p. 39.
60. Dunne, 1973, abstract.

61. Nelson, 1975.

62. Steffensen, 1975, p. 110.

63. Bell, 1975, p. 99.

64. Hite and Drummond, 1975.

65. Hawley and Vallanti, 1970.

66. Ibid.; Smith et al., 1974.

67. Edelfelt, Corwin, and Hanna, 1974.

68. Washington, 1964, p. 5.

69. Ibid., introduction.

70. Ibid.

71. Washington, D.C. Public Schools, 1968.

72. Ibid., p. 3.

73. Ibid.

74. Ibid., p. 4.

75. Washington School of Psychiatry, 1968.

76. National Advisory Council on Education Professions Development, 1975.

77. Hite and Drummond, 1975.

78. Nelson, 1975, p. 98.

79. *Journal of Teacher Education*, 1975, p. 113.

80. Washington School of Psychiatry, 1968, p. 38.

81. Steffensen, 1975, p. 110.

82. Edelfelt, Corwin, and Hanna, 1974, p. 11.

83. Hite and Drummond, 1975, p. 133.

84. National Advisory Council on Education Professions Development, 1975.

85. Smith et al., 1974.

86. Bigelow, 1971.

87. Davies in Bigelow, 1971, p. xi.

88. University of Virginia, Evaluation Research Center, 1973a.

89. Smith et al., 1974.

90. Hawley and Vallanti, 1970.

91. University of Virginia, Evaluation Research Center, 1973b.

92. Ibid., p. 45.

93. University of Virginia, Evaluation Research Center, 1973b.

94. Ibid.

95. Ibid.

96. Perrone, 1989.

97. Crockett et al., 1969.

98. Vito Perrone, in an interview with the author 7 December 1989, noted that the assessment was historically correct although lacking the narrative element that would amplify it. Larry Cuban, who was a member of the President's Advisory Council on the National Teacher Corps, also confirmed in a letter to the author, dated 18 December 1989, that the assessment given here corresponds to the advice the Council gave to Richard Graham, then Director of the National Teacher Corps.

99. National Advisory Council on Education Professions Development, 1975.

100. Clear and Edgar, 1970, p. 45.

101. Edelfelt, Corwin, and Hanna, 1974.

102. Arth and Wagoner, 1969, p. 801.

103. Edelfelt, Corwin, and Hanna, 1974, p. 12.

104. *Journal of Teacher Education*, 1975, p. 113.

105. Clear and Edgar, 1970; Dunne, 1973.

106. Bell, 1975, p. 99.

107. Nelson, 1975, p. 99; National Advisory Council on Education Professions Development, 1975; Edelfelt, Corwin, and Hanna, 1974.

108. Marsh, 1975.

109. National Advisory Council on Education Professions Development, 1975.

110. Hite and Drummond, 1975.

111. Edelfelt, Corwin, and Hanna, 1974, p. 13.

Chapter 2

1. Ravitch, 1983.

2. Grant, 1979. See, for example, Fisher, 1978.

3. Houston, 1987, p. 156.

4. White, 1973, p. 309.

5. Hernandez, 1974, p. 3.

6. Houston, 1987, p. 316.

7. Riessman, 1976, p. ix.

8. Stinnett, 1971, notes in the introduction to *Unfinished Business of the Teaching Profession in the 1970's* that voters turned down school budgets in 20% of New York's 700 school districts in 1969, the highest rejection rate ever.

9. Ravitch, 1974; Davidson, 1973; Rossmiller, 1979.

10. Spratlen, 1973.

11. Rossmiller, 1979; Schiff, 1976; Borman and Spring, 1984.

12. Hernandez, 1974, p. 3.

13. West, 1973.

14. Colquit, 1978, p. 198.

15. Ravitch, 1983, p. 268; Epps, 1979, p. 112. See also Tyack, 1974; Bastian et al., 1986; Katznelson and Weir, 1985; Levine and Levine, 1970; Cremin, 1988. Gerald Grace, 1984, notes that urban education as subject of inquiry took institutional shape in the 1960s, so it is understandable that the political issues of the day would be reflected in the scholarship.

16. Stinnett, 1971, p. 2.

17. Ornstein, 1981.

18. Schiff, 1976, p. 426.

19. Jencks, 1973, p. 103. In this special section of the *Harvard Educational Review*, issued as no. 8 in the reprint series, Jencks answered critics of an earlier work, Jencks et al., 1972.

20. Cooper, 1984.

21. Jencks et al., 1973, p. 256.

22. Riessman, 1976, p. 72.

23. Ibid., p. 105.

24. Ibid., p. 121.

25. For an informative, pithy exchange, see Shanker, 1969, and Zeluck, 1969. Diane Ravitch, 1974, in a recapitulation of events that confirms Shanker's version, describes the strike at length in *The Great School Wars: New York City 1805–1973*; Ira Glasser, 1969, author of the report issued by the New York Civil Liberties Union, analyzes events as Zeluck presents them, in "The Burden of Blame: A Report on the Ocean Hill–Brownsville School Controversy."

26. Grant, 1979.

27. See Rogers, 1968, for the most comprehensive examination of the New York City Board of Education's response to efforts to integrate city schools. Rogers's study was completed about a year before the Ocean Hill–Brownsville strike.

28. The controversy over the More Effective Schools (MES) program is an important but neglected aspect of the Ocean Hill–Brownsville strike. *The Urban Review*, 1968, contains a description of the program and results of the evaluation conducted by the Center for Urban Education, as well as rebuttals by one independent source and the MES director of evaluation. See also Channon, 1967, for an earlier first-person account of one MES site.

29. White, 1973, p. 310. Diane Ravitch, 1968, defended the opposite point of view, studying four private programs known for their educational excellence. She concluded that compensatory programs succeeded when they duplicated the educational conditions that were conventional in leading public and private schools.

30. Cohen, 1968.

31. Ibid.

32. For example, Floyd T. Waterman, 1974, warned that some programs claiming to be CBTE-driven were not identified by education students as having any CBTE component.

33. Houston, 1987, p. 44.

34. Houston and Howsam, 1972, foreword.

35. Sandefur and Nicklas, 1981, p. 747.

36. National Advisory Council on Education Professions Development, 1976, pp. 6–7.

37. Hilbert, 1982, p. 393.

38. Travers, 1974, p. 3.

39. Tarr, 1973.

40. Ibid.

41. Roth, 1972.

42. Houston and Howsam, 1972, pp. 1–16.

43. Ornstein and Talmage, Spring 1973.

44. White, 1973, p. 311.

45. Washington School of Psychiatry, 1968, p. 38.

46. Weiner, 1976.

47. Shanker, 1977, p. 2.

48. Kemble and McKenna, 1975, introduction.

49. Ibid., p. 8

50. Ibid., p. 17.

51. Ibid., p. 29.

52. Ornstein and Talmage, July 1973, p. 136.

53. Ibid., p. 149; Houston and Howsam, 1972, foreword; "The Teacher Corps Concept," 1975.

54. Nelson, 1975, p. 98; Bauch, 1970.

55. Otten, 1973.

56. Hernandez, 1974, pp. 17–18.

57. Hunt, 1974, p. 28.

58. Hilliard, 1974, p. 42.

59. Hernandez, 1974, p. 6.

60. This basic conflict is discussed, but without explicit reference to CBTE and multicultural education, in Morgan, 1979.

61. Powell, 1980.

62. *The Urban Review*, 1967.

63. Gage, 1972, p. 27.

64. Medley, Soar, and Soar, 1975, p. 22.

65. Andrews, 1972; Rosenshine and Furst, 1971; Travers, 1974; National Advisory Council on Education Professions Development, 1976.

66. Gage, 1972, p. 28.

67. Stern and Harter, 1981.

68. Cazden, 1976, p. 75.

69. Metz, 1978, p. 144.

70. Ibid., p. 20.

71. For a comprehensive discussion of urban school bureaucracy see Goodman, 1977. Also, *The Urban Review*, 1981, summarized research in ERIC/ CUE on reforming the large urban high school. A few writers continued to discuss the importance of reforming urban school systems to permit community and parent participation. See Davies, 1981. However, scholarship on reforming urban schools to encourage community participation was rarely joined to a discussion of teacher performance, as Metz and Goodman attempted. Also, Larry Cuban, 1982, analyzed the social and school influences that historically shaped teaching styles, in a study later expanded into a book.

72. Ralph and Fennessey, 1983; Cooper, 1984.

73. Edmonds, 1984, p. 61.

74. Ibid., p. 57.

75. Brandt, 1982.

76. Ibid.

77. Edmonds, 1984, p. 62.

78. Ibid., p. 64.

79. Ibid.

80. Ibid., p. 62.

81. Brandt, 1982, p. 14.

82. Ibid.

83. Brandt, 1982.

84. Laura Cooper argued there were two, incompatible strands in the effective schools literature, Edmonds's model being one, and Brookover and Rutter's the other. It was Edmonds's work that was applied to urban schools, however, so I have discussed his model alone. Cooper concluded that Edmonds's reliance on centralized authority to direct reform, as opposed to Brookover and Rutter's emphasis on the individual school developing and acting on values developed over time, was a less helpful strategy. My experience with the School Improvement Plan (SIP) of Martin Luther King High School in New York City confirms Cooper's observations. After months of meetings, the committee arrived at several helpful suggestions for improving the school, but not a single one of its recommendations could be implemented because of either fiscal restraints, Board of Education regulations, or state requirements. The SIP committee was mandated and funded because of King students' poor performance on state and city tests, but these tests imposed a curricular straightjacket on every department except for English. The mandate to create a plan to improve the school ended with the creation of the plan and contained no provisions to assist school committees to carry out their ideas, so in the end King's SIP ultimately discouraged and frustrated school personnel who participated in its formulation.

Chapter 3

1. National Commission on Excellence in Education, 1983.
2. Yeakey and Johnston, 1985, p. 157.
3. Howe, 1984, p. 3.
4. Johnson, 1989.
5. Prakash, 1986, p. 217.
6. National Commission on Excellence in Education, 1983; Timar and Kirp, 1988, p. 13.
7. Weiner, May 1990.
8. Carnegie Forum on Education and the Economy, 1986, p. 2.
9. Ibid., p. 107.
10. Spring, 1984; Finkelstein, 1984, p. 275.
11. Dreeban, 1987, p. 359.
12. Cohen and Neufeld, 1981; Kearns, 1989.
13. Bastian et al., 1986, p. 4.
14. Toch, 1984.
15. Borman and Spring, 1984, p. 7.
16. Levin, 1986.
17. Carnegie Foundation for the Advancement of Teaching, 1988, prologue.
18. Ibid.
19. Mark and Anderson, 1984.
20. Howe, 1983, 1984.
21. See Boyer, 1983, a report issued for the Carnegie Foundation for the Advancement of Teaching, and Sizer, 1984. Their studies reflected and encour-

aged policy concerns about secondary school curricula and organization. While many of Sizer's recommendations contradicted the major reform proposals, it is interesting to compare these two volumes with the kinds of scholarship undertaken as schools were desegregating. For instance, see Heath, 1983, for an examination of children's language acquisition in three different communities and its ramifications for school success.

22. Clark, Astuto, and Rooney, 1983, p. 188.

23. Verstegen and Clark, 1988, p. 134.

24. Verstegen and Clark, 1988.

25. Piccigallo, 1989.

26. One exception was Ira Shor's work. See Shor, 1986, 1987.

27. Clark, Astuto, and Rooney, 1983.

28. Kirp, 1986, p. 3.

29. Guthrie, 1990, p. 34.

30. A bipartisan group of senators introduced S. 1675, a bill to resurrect the Teacher Corps, to the 101st Congress. Its scope is considerably smaller than the original project, however.

31. Holmes, 1990.

32. Odden, 1984, p. 311.

33. Timar and Kirp, 1988.

34. Haberman, 1987, p. 16.

35. Kerr, 1983, p. 531.

36. Ibid., p. 528.

37. The most widely debated reports were issued by the Holmes Group, NCATE, and the Carnegie Task Force on Teaching as a Profession, according to an assessment by Tom, 1987.

38. Prakash, 1986.

39. American Association of Colleges for Teacher Education, 1987; Baratz, 1987; Darling-Hammond et al., 1987.

40. Graham, 1987. Michael Sedlak and Steven Schlossman, 1986, present the point of view that dominated discourse about the issue.

41. This is most apparent in *A Nation Prepared*, which contains a scenario describing how schools will, or at least should, be organized in the twenty-first century.

42. Edmonds, 1984.

43. Seeley, 1982.

44. Don Davies, 1987, refers to it as an "ecological" approach; James Comer et al., 1986, also used the word *ecological* to describe the approach to school reform advocated in Comer's School Development Program. In an earlier article Comer, 1975, referred to the approach as "holistic." David Seeley, 1984, distinguishes "educational partnership" from "service delivery."

45. Carnegie Forum on Education and the Economy, 1986; The Holmes Group, 1986; National Commission for Excellence in Teacher Education, 1985; Shanker, 1985; National Education Association, 1982.

46. Dreeban, 1987, p. 363.

47. Powell, 1980.

48. Shulman, 1987, p. 4. Powell, 1980, traces the perennial controversies about professionalizing teaching. One of the themes in Stinnett, 1971, was that teaching had to become a real profession by taking control over standards for admission, preparation, licensure, professional growth, and continuance in practice.

49. Wright, 1988.

50. *The Urban Review*, 1968. Shanker's discussion of national certification illuminates how professionalization necessarily excludes significant community or parental participation in schools.

51. Sykes, 1986, p. 366.

52. Graham, 1984, p. 55.

53. Wise, Darling-Hammond, and Berry, 1987.

54. Carnegie Forum on Education and the Economy, 1986; Darling-Hammond and Berry, 1988; National Research Council, 1988; Sedlak and Schlossman, 1986; Wise, Darling-Hammond, and Berry, 1987; Shulman, 1987.

55. Proposals for "school governance" or "school-based management" varied widely. Those which made parents partners in school governance, according to my categories, belong under the ecological approach. In contrast, Susan Moore Johnson, 1989, includes only teachers and administrators in her concept of shared governance, adding that parents might be involved in rethinking school purposes so teachers don't feel as isolated and unsupported; however, parents' participation would clearly be tangential to the real exercise of authority by teachers and administrators. Parental involvement is even more peripheral in Albert Shanker's proposal for restructured schools, outlined in Shanker, 1985. In the Shanker/AFT plan, parents and students would be given a choice of school but governance of each school would be controlled by teachers.

56. Carnegie Forum on Education and the Economy, 1986, p. 55.

57. The Holmes Group, 1986, p. 40.

58. The reports differed over which of the profession's segments should regulate entry. The Holmes Group would give research universities control of standards through a series of teacher examinations. The National Committee for Excellence in Teacher Education would give state government the control over standards but argued that the task should then be delegated in the main to education professionals, presumably including representatives of schools of education. The NEA advocated autonomous state agencies governed by a majority of K–12 teachers, all of them NEA members, to approve teacher preparation programs and administer a test. None of the proposals addressed the fact that each plan gave control over entry to the group authoring the report.

59. The Holmes Group, 1986; Carnegie Forum on Education and the Economy, 1986; National Commission on Excellence in Teacher Education, 1985.

60. Shanker, 1985.

61. Raywid, 1987, p. 414.

62. Dreeban, 1987.

63. Raywid, 1987, p. 416.

64. Bullough and Gitlin, 1985, p. 220. Martin Haberman, 1987, argues

that the country's 120 largest school districts have the worst problems of bu-
reaucratization.

65. Haberman, 1988, p. 23.
66. Haberman, 1988.
67. Tewel, 1988, p. 39.
68. Perrone, 1985, p. 645.
69. Bereiter, 1985, p. 540.
70. Ibid., p. 538.
71. Slavin and Madden, 1989.
72. Bastian et al., 1986.
73. National Coalition of Advocates for Students, 1986.
74. Levin, 1986, introduction, n.p.
75. Gilbert and Gay, 1985, p. 134.
76. Schneider, 1990. The discussant, William Boyd, remarked after the
presentation that identifying families as "deficient" echoed the earlier "repug-
nant" error of labeling students as deficient rather than culturally different.
77. Bryk and Thum, 1989.
78. Grant, 1989, p. 769.

Chapter 4

1. Cochran-Smith and Lytle, 1990; Lortie, 1973, p. 484.
2. Commins and Miramontes, 1989.
3. Roberts, 1970.
4. Smith, 1991.
5. Although teacher unionism became institutionalized in this form, in its
earliest years its self-definition was far different, or at least far more ambiguous. The paradigm counterposed to the service delivery model, which made
teacher unionism a special interest group, was a conceptualization of teacher
unionism as a segment of a broad social movement committed to improving
public education. Maxine Greene defended this alternative paradigm, which I
explain fully in two articles, Weiner, 1976, 1987.
6. Greene, 1967, p. 671.
7. For a thoughtful analysis of this process, see Labaree, 1992.
8. Fine, 1986.
9. Ibid. In addition, Ana Maria Villegas, 1988, argues that the sociolin-
guistic literature on home–school language disjunctures excludes consideration
of social inequalities that sustain the school failure of minority students and
thus doom school improvement efforts. A few other researchers, like Sara Lawrence Lightfoot, have investigated relationships between families and schools
and conditions in urban schools, contributing to our understanding of the social
context of urban schooling, so the studies described in this section are not
presented as an exclusive listing of relevant scholarship. What is clear, however, is that there is no *body* of work in which scholars have discussed one
another's findings, to challenge or refine them.

10. Rogers, 1968.
11. Fordham and Ogbu, 1986.
12. DiLeonardo, 1990, p. 672.
13. Oakes, 1982.
14. Goldenberg and Gallimore, 1991.
15. Payne, 1984.
16. Rosenbaum, Kulieke, and Rubinowitz, 1988.
17. Bryk and Thum, 1989.
18. Kennedy, Spring 1991.

Chapter 5

1. See Holusha, 1990. Holusha reports that many economists, scholars, executives, and other experts on American industrial policy argue that financial manipulations, such as G.E.'s purchase of its own stock, are sapping the nation's global competitiveness by diverting expenditures from basic research. In another article in the business pages, Joselow, 1989, the chief economist for a bank in Providence, Rhode Island, the national costume jewelry manufacturing capital, argued that low productivity in the industry was due to management's "productivity sins," such as poor scheduling of workers and arrival of raw materials, or the layout of production lines.

2. A contrasting view of productivity, educational attainment of the work force, and the nation's economic competitiveness is given in Center for Popular Economics, 1986. Harvey J. Graff, 1987, contends that economic growth and education are not necessarily "sequential" or "collateral" (p. 65), pointing to Sweden and Scotland as examples of societies that achieved near-universal literacy before the nineteenth century yet remained desperately poor.

3. Fine, 1986, p. 397. The material in this article is expanded in Fine, 1991.

4. Fine's work confirms one of Richard Murnane's conclusions. Murnane, 1992, argues that the educational achievement of the work force can improve productivity, but also notes that the economy's operation dampens the academic achievement of minority students in inner city schools when they have little chance of finding good-paying jobs, even with a high school diploma.

5. Fine, 1986, p. 399.

6. Ibid.

7. Cohen and Neufeld, 1981; Bastian et al., 1986.

8. Gutmann, 1987. As discussed in Chapter 3, this critical role of education has been slighted in the major reform proposals since 1983. Bastian et al., 1986, argue that not only does it deserve as much consideration as education's economic usefulness, but it is actually the cause of the malaise in nonurban and urban schools. What is at the root of public education's failures is a "crisis of citizenship" that has made education's constituencies passive clients. Urban education's noneconomic purposes are not explicitly discussed in this study because they are assumed to be the same for the entire society.

9. See Aronowitz and Giroux, 1985, for the philosophical and political underpinning of this idea; it is applied directly to teacher preparation in a textbook for prospective teachers by Giroux, Penna, and Pinar, 1981; a condensed version of this analysis was written by Giroux and McLaren, 1986. Ira Shor, 1986, offers a similar analysis of the appropriate role of teacher education.

10. Giroux and McLaren, 1986, p. 236.

11. Gordon, 1985, argues that teacher educators should teach critical consciousness, using the methodological accounts of teachers practicing an emancipatory pedagogy.

12. Shor, 1986, p. 413.

13. Freire, 1982, p. 103.

14. Ibid., p. 40.

15. Brickman, 1964b, p. 83. Dewey's essays originally appeared in the *New Republic* between 1920 and 1928.

16. Ibid., p. 87.

17. Ibid., p. 100. Dewey's understanding of Lenin's critique of educational reform's relation to politics is confirmed by several passages in Lenin's collected works, 1965. For example, Lenin argued that his New Economic Program depended on eradicating illiteracy because "the illiterate person stands outside politics. . . .Without that there can be no politics" but only "rumors, gossip, fairy tales, and prejudices, but not politics" (*Collected Works* 33, p. 78).

18. In Wilson, 1928, the author describes, uncritically, the Bolsheviks' initial transformation of the educational system; Brickman, 1964a, traces how the Soviet government's political changes from the mid-1920s through the 1930s paralleled revisions of school curricula and organization, as well as Dewey's official loss of prestige; Hein, 1975, describes the evolution of "open schools" in the Soviet Union and their precipitous decline under Stalin. He argues that Stalin's rule could not tolerate the "spirit of investigation and looseness" that characterized the early reforms inspired by Dewey's work (p. 112).

19. Liston and Zeichner, 1987. Although Liston and Zeichner advocate a critical pedagogy for teacher education, they define it as moral education and criticize the writers who blur the distinction between teacher as activist and teacher as educator.

20. Dewey, 1904; Liston and Zeichner, 1991.

21. Kennedy, 1989, p. 19.

22. Liston and Zeichner, 1991.

23. Zeichner, 1991, p. 374.

24. Liston and Zeichner, 1991, p. 39.

25. For a more complete analysis of this idea, see Draper, Summer 1990.

26. For an instructive analysis of the limitations of models of reflective inquiry, see Liston and Zeichner, 1991.

27. For a comprehensive critique, see Welker, 1992.

28. Wise, Darling-Hammond, and Berry, 1987.

29. Lipsky, 1980.

30. Ibid., p. 76.
31. Little, 1987.
32. Barr and Dreeban, 1983.
33. Ginsberg, Schwartz, Olson, and Bennett, 1986.
34. Lipsky, 1980, p. 202.
35. Ibid., p. 203.
36. Ibid., p. 204.
37. Comer, 1987, p. 14.
38. Lipsky outlines his recommendations for reform in chapter 13 of his book; Comer describes his program at length in *School Power*, 1980. He also describes his program in New Haven, later applied in Benton Harbor, Michigan, and his theories in a paper presented at the American Psychological Association, Comer et al., 1986, and two articles, Comer, 1984, 1987.
39. Comer et al., 1986, p. 11.
40. Comer, 1984.
41. Comer, 1987, p. 14.
42. Comer et al., 1986.
43. Comer, 1980, p. 69.
44. Comer et al., 1986, p. 9
45. Comer, 1980; Barth, 1972. Barth does not identify the name of his school or district in his account of the project, but several incidents that he describes, as well as the program's location and affiliations, identify the site. In discussing his work with me on 20 April 1990, Barth confirmed that he was a principal in the Comer-Yale-New Haven School District project during its first year.
46. Comer, 1980, p. 20.
47. Barth, 1972, p. 207.
48. Educators who are unfamiliar with Barth's work may find Comer's description of his first project in New Haven complete, because Comer acknowledges that the program had serious problems. For instance, Charles Payne, 1984, makes this error, commending Comer for detailing all the "misfires and misunderstanding . . . the stuff of real life!" (p. 169). Barth's account strongly suggests that not all sides of the misunderstandings are presented accurately.
49. Comer, 1987, p. 207.
50. Ibid.
51. Ibid.
52. Comer, 1980.
53. Comer, 1987, p. 14.
54. Katz, 1987.
55. Kaestle, 1973, p. 178.
56. Cohen and Neufeld, 1981.
57. Cuban, 1987.
58. See, for instance, information about the Kent State University M.A.T. program initiated with Akron Central-Hower High School in The Holmes Group, 1989.

Chapter 6

1. Smith et al., 1969, p. 27.
2. Liston and Zeichner, 1991.
3. Ogbu, 1989, p. 196.
4. Adelman, 1970.
5. Ibid.
6. Paley, 1979, p. xv.
7. Ibid.
8. Ibid, xi.
9. Balman, 1981.

10. It is interesting to note that the researchers did not indicate how their experience as teachers in the school system influenced their understanding of conditions, but because these researchers were all well acquainted with New York City Board of Education policies, they were, in the language of contemporary researchers, privy to "local knowledge."

11. Roberts, 1970.
12. Sarason, Davidson, and Blatt, 1986.
13. Smith et al., 1969, p. 19.
14. Ibid., p. 5.

15. One result of this collision between student needs and systemic rigidity is the staggering growth of special education programs. *Newsday* reported that one out of every eight students in New York City public schools is enrolled in special education classes; see Chiles, 1990.

16. Grant, 1989.
17. McDiarmid, 1992.
18. Kennedy, November 1991.

19. See Quality Education for Minorities Project, 1990. Appendix B briefly describes some of these differences, noting also that low-income whites face many of the educational barriers that confront the minority groups discussed in the report.

20. Private conversation, Dr. Charles Sklar, assistant professor of pediatrics at New York University, 14 March 1990, New York City.

21. Menand, 1992, p. 84.
22. Liston and Zeichner, 1991, p. 39.
23. Ibid., pp. 37–118.
24. Ibid., p. 87.

25. Zimpher, 1989, provides the demographic profile of teacher candidates. Haberman, 1987, observes that because most schools of education are removed from cities, teachers are graduated who have no contact with urban schools or students.

26. Sedlak and Schlossman, 1986, p. 34. These authors do not pinpoint when this transition occurred, nor do they discuss urban teachers specifically. Since Haberman provides no empirical data to support his contention that most teacher-candidates have no experience in urban schooling, and my research has not turned up any city-by-city survey that identifies the geographic and

class origins of urban teachers, I cannot determine exactly who teaches now in the nation's urban centers. The proportions may well vary from one urban center to another and may change dramatically in a short time, altered by certification requirements, for instance. The City University has trained over half of New York City's 65,000 teachers. (See Weiss, 1990.) In 1988–1989, according to a report of a CUNY task force on secondary education, only 89 teachers were certified in secondary education *in the entire CUNY* system because of changes in state policies that allowed the city to hire uncertified teachers.

27. Powell, 1980; Elisberg, 1981.

28. Kelman, 1974, p. 69. Kelman's work takes up the Wesleyan program from the standpoint of the students' needs as teachers, whereas Faith Weinstein Dunne's 1973 dissertation, also based on her work at Wesleyan, took up the question of preparing students to be change agents. Dunne's work also addressed the specific problems of "M.A.T. types," who differed from the average urban teacher in class, ambition, and achievement.

29. In his description of stages of development, Robert Kegan, 1982, notes that when an individual assumes the "institutional self" of adulthood, an important issue is "assumption of authority" and assuming a "career . . . rather than having a job" (p. 227). Kegan's theory fits perfectly with Kelman's observations about how the M.A.T. program's expressed goal of training educational leaders sabotaged the participants' success as teachers. Using Kegan's framework to explain the problem, the M.A.T. student's need to adjust to the "institutional self" when he or she began work as a teacher, for instance, by deciding how to adjust to school policies, was undercut by the knowledge that teaching was *not* the real career but a preliminary hurdle.

30. Dow, 1979, p. 2.

31. Ibid., p. 11.

32. Sedlak and Schlossman, 1986. Part of the difficulty is that teachers and their history were ignored by historians until rather recently, as I discuss in a paper presented at the American Educational Research Association, April 1990.

33. Association of Teacher Educators, 1986, p. v.

34. Brown, 1978; Needham, 1973; Courts, 1983.

35. Weiner, 1989, October 1990.

36. Private conversation with Fern Lowenfels, 7 June 1990, New York City.

37. George H. Eastman, 1963, traces this progression, noting that Dewey never explicitly disavowed his earlier idea. The quote is taken from Dewey's "Pedagogy as a University Discipline," published in 1896 while he headed the Department of Pedagogy and developed the Lab School.

38. Dewey, 1904, p. 16.

39. Ibid., p. 23.

40. Ibid., p. 24.

41. Cremin, 1977, p. 19.

42. Sizer, 1984; Powell, Farrar, and Cohen, 1985.

43. Newmann, 1985, p. 190. Vito Perrone, 1985, comments that the cur-

riculum in urban high schools today appears very much as it has been for most of the past 50 years, with textbooks maintaining a tight grip.

44. Oakes, 1982, notes that in lower tracks, classrooms are more characterized by "primitive and hostile relationships between teachers and students and between students and their peers" (p. 118).

45. Final examination of B.M., a student in EDS 302, College of Staten Island, spring 1990.

46. Final examination of N.M., a student in EDS 302, College of Staten Island, spring 1990.

47. These differences are explored in detail in Weiner, 1989.

48. One of my supervisors, whenever he hosted visitors, exemplified this dichotomy between what schools of education consider appropriate practice and what urban school systems expect from teachers. He avoided showing my classes to his superiors from the Board of Education, but anyone from a school of education was taken immediately to observe me. Similarly, as part of a practicum in an English methods course I taught at the College of Staten Island, my students appreciated observing one teacher who used student-centered or collaborative learning techniques. Subsequently I learned he was being pressured by the principal to make his classes more traditional.

49. Cuban, 1970.

50. Haberman, 1987.

51. Weiner, October 1990. Research is under way at Jersey City State College to compare the effects of urban field experiences on elementary and secondary students.

52. Sandholtz, 1990.

53. One counselor was assigned to four classes in the wealthy Westchester high school I taught in. Julia Richman High School had one counselor for every 400 students, and the problems that students had were far more severe.

54. Fine, 1991, describes how New York City high schools are organized into tiers, the demographics resulting from competitive exams to get into high school and funding policies that penalize schools with high proportions of students requiring remedial work.

55. Weiner, October 1990.

56. Grant, 1989. Martin Haberman, 1988, proposes a mandatory paid internship for urban teachers, an idea that is not new. In *City Training Schools for Teachers* Frank Manny, 1915, noted that city training schools paid teachers for a year of practice teaching to compensate for time spent in preparation that would otherwise have been spent working and earning money in another occupation. The sum paid was, however, more "a subsidy than a salary" (p. 63).

57. Glazer, 1974; Haberman, 1987.

58. Weiner, October 1990. Urban student interns identified the university supervisor as the most important link between their campus training and their school site experience.

59. This phrase comes from Marilyn Cochran-Smith, 1991.

60. Haberman, 1987.

Bibliography

Adams, Raymond S., Karuna Ahmad, and Robert Jameson. "Sociology and the Training of Teachers of the Disadvantaged." U.S. Office of Education Contract No. OEG 09-354719-1712-725. 1969.

Adams, Raymond S., Nicholas J. Sobin, and Gloria Lockerman. "Linguistics and the Training of Teachers of the Disadvantaged." U.S. Office of Education Contract No. OEG 09-354719-1712-725. University of Missouri, Columbia, 1969.

Adelman, Howard S. *Teacher Education and the Disadvantaged: Some Basic Issues and Some Partial Answers.* Los Angeles: California State Department of Education, 1970.

American Association of Colleges for Teacher Education. *Minority Teacher Recruitment and Retention: A Call for Action.* Washington, DC: American Association of Colleges for Teacher Education, 1987.

Andrews, Theodore E. "Certifications." In *Competency-Based Teacher Education: Progress, Problems, and Prospects,* edited by Robert W. Houston and Robert B. Howsam. Chicago: Science Research Associates, Inc., 1972.

Aronowitz, Stanley, and Henry A. Giroux. *Education Under Siege.* Boston: Bergin and Garvey, 1985.

Arth, Alfred A., and Jennings L. Wagoner, Jr. "Teacher Corps Interns: A Different Breed." *Educational Leadership* 26 (May 1969): 801–805.

Association of Teacher Educators. *Competency Based Teacher Education—A Potpourri of Perspectives.* Washington, DC: Association of Teacher Educators, 1974.

Association of Teacher Educators. *Guidelines for Professional Experiences in Teacher Education.* Reston, VA: Association of Teacher Educators, 1986.

Ayers, William. "Fact or Fancy: The Knowledge Base Quest in Teacher Education." *Journal of Teacher Education* 39 (September–October 1988): 25–28.

Balman, Lynne Susan Watzke. "A Follow-Up of the Nature of Student Teacher Transference of Special Experiences From a University Teacher-Training Center to the Urban Public Classroom." Ed.D. diss., Wayne State University, 1981.

Baratz, Joan C. "Black Participation in the Teacher Pool." Paper prepared for the Carnegie Forum on Education and the Economy, January, 1987.

Barr, Rebecca, and Robert Dreeben. *How Schools Work.* Chicago: Univ. of Chicago Press, 1983.

Barth, Roland S. *Open Education and the American School*. New York: Aga-
   thon Press, 1972.
Bastian, Ann, Norman Fruchter, Marilyn Gittell, Colin Greer, and Kenneth
   Haskins. *Choosing Equality: The Case for Democratic Schooling*. Phila-
   delphia: Temple Univ. Press, 1986.
Bauch, Jerold P. "Community Participation in Teacher Education: Teacher
   Corps and the Model Programs." Athens: Georgia University, 1970. ERIC
   Document Reproduction Service No. ED 042 700.
Bell, Terrell H. "The Progress of the Teacher Corps." *Journal of Teacher Edu-
   cation* 26 (Summer 1975): 99–100.
Bereiter, Carl. "The Changing Face of Educational Disadvantagement." *Phi
   Delta Kappan* 66 (April 1985): 538–541.
Berube, Martin. "Teachers and the Urban School Crisis." In *The Urban School
   Crisis*, edited by League for Industrial Democracy and United Federation
   of Teachers. New York: League for Industrial Democracy and United
   Federation of Teachers, 1966.
Bigelow, Donald N., ed. *The Liberal Arts and Teacher Education. A Confron-
   tation*. Lincoln: Univ. of Nebraska Press, 1971.
Bird, Tom, and Judith Warren Little. "How Schools Organize the Teaching
   Occupation." *Elementary School Journal* 86 (March 1986): 493–511.
Borman, Kathryn M., and Joel H. Spring. *Schools in Central Cities: Structure
   and Process*. New York: Longman, 1984.
Bossone, Richard M., ed. *What Works in Urban Schools*. Proceedings from the
   First Conference of the University/Urban Schools National Task Force,
   New Orleans, October 1981. Published by the Center for Advanced Study
   in Education, City University of New York.
Boyer, Ernest L. *High School*. New York: Harper & Row, 1983.
Brandt, Ronald. "On School Improvement: A Conversation with Ronald Ed-
   monds." *Educational Leadership* 40 (December 1982): 13–15.
Brickman, William. "Soviet Attitudes Toward John Dewey as an Educator."
   In *John Dewey and the World View*, edited by Douglas E. Lawson and
   Arthur E. Lean. Carbondale: Southern Illinois Univ. Press, 1964a.
Brickman, William W., ed. *John Dewey's Impressions of Soviet Russia and
   the Revolutionary World: Mexico, China, Turkey*. New York: Teachers
   College Press, 1964b. (Original edition published by New Republic,
   1929).
Brickman, William W., and Stanley Lehrer. *John Dewey: Master Educator*.
   N.p. Society for the Advancement of Education, 1961.
Brinkley, Alan. "Writing the History of Contemporary America: Dilemmas
   and Challenges." *Daedalus* 113 (Summer 1984): 121–142.
Brown, Robert Maffett. "The Effect of an Urban School Field Experience
   on the Attitudes of Preservice Elementary School Teachers." D.Ed. diss.,
   Pennsylvania State University, 1978.
Bryk, Anthony S., and Yeow Meng Thum. "The Effects of High School Organi-
   zation on Dropping Out: An Exploratory Investigation." *American Educa-
   tional Research Journal* 26 (Fall 1989): 353–385.
Bullough, Robert V., Jr., and Andrew D. Gitlin. "Schooling and Change: A

View from the Lower Rung." *Teachers College Record* 87 (Winter 1985): 219–237.

Callahan, Raymond E. *Education and the Cult of Efficiency.* Chicago: Univ. of Chicago Press, 1962.

Campbell, Richard. "Basic Competences and Characteristics of the Successful Urban Teacher." Paper presented at the annual meeting of the Association of Teacher Educators, Orlando, Florida, January 1983.

Carnegie Forum on Education and the Economy. *A Nation Prepared: Teachers for the Twenty-First Century. Report of the Task Force on Teaching as a Profession.* Washington, DC: Carnegie Forum on Education and the Economy, 1986.

Carnegie Foundation for the Advancement of Teaching. *An Imperiled Generation: Saving Urban Schools.* Washington, DC: Carnegie Foundation for the Advancement of Teaching, 1988.

Carter, Carol J. "A Study and Clinical Analysis of Trainer of Teacher Trainers: The Preparation of Educational Leaders for Urban Inner City Schools." Ed.D. diss., University of Massachusetts, 1971.

Castelli, Albert Louis. "A Study of the Responses of Inner City Teachers of Disadvantaged Children to a Questionnaire on Possible Components of a Preparation Program for Teachers of Disadvantaged Children." Ed.D. diss., Wayne State University, 1968.

Castro, Janet. "Untapped Verbal Fluency of Black Schoolchildren." In *The Culture of Poverty: A Critique,* edited by Eleanor Leacock. New York: Simon & Schuster, 1971.

Cazden, Courtney B. "How Knowledge about Language Helps the Classroom Teacher—Or Does It?" *The Urban Review* 9 (Summer 1976): 72–90.

Center for Popular Economics. *Economic Report of the People.* Boston: South End Press, 1986.

Chaney, John S. "An Analysis of Public School Teacher Strikes in the United States 1966–1968." *Urban Education* 8 (July 1973): 179–194.

Channon, Gloria. "The More Effective Schools." *The Urban Review* 2 (February 1967): 23–36.

Chiles, Nick. "Fernandez Asks Lifting of Mandate for Disabled." *Newsday,* 25 May 1990, p. 6.

City University of New York Task Force on Education Programs and Curriculum Impact. City University of New York, October 1988. Photocopy.

Clark, David L., Terry A. Astuto, and Paula M. Rooney. "The Changing Structure of Federal Education Policy in the 1980's." *Phi Delta Kappan* 65 (November 1983): 188–193.

Clear, Delbert K., and Donald E. Edgar. "Training Change Agents in the Public School Context." Paper presented at the annual meeting of the American Educational Research Association, Minneapolis, March 1970. ERIC Document Reproduction Service No. ED 039 178.

Cleveland State University, College of Education. *The Urban Connection in Teacher Education.* Cleveland: Cleveland State Univ., 1976.

Cochran-Smith, Marilyn. "Learning to Teach Against the Grain." *Harvard Educational Review* 61 (August 1991): 279–310.

Cochran-Smith, Marilyn, and Susan Lytle. "Research on Teaching and Teacher Research: The Issues that Divide." *Educational Researcher* 19 (March 1990): 2–11.

Cohen, David K. "Teachers Want What Children Need—Or Do They?" *The Urban Review* 2 (June 1968): 25–29.

Cohen, David K., and Barbara Neufeld. "The Failure of High Schools and the Progress of Education." *Daedalus* 110 (Summer 1981): 69–90.

Cole, Stephen. *The Unionization of Teachers.* New York: Praeger, 1969.

Colquit, Jesse L. "The Teacher's Dilemma in Facilitating the Black Experience." *The Journal of Negro Education* 48 (Spring 1978): 192–200.

Comer, James P. "Black Education: A Holistic View." *The Urban Review* 8 (Fall 1975): 162–170.

Comer, James P. *School Power.* New York: Free Press, 1980.

Comer, James P. "Home-School Relationships as They Affect the Academic Success of Children." *Education and Urban Society* 16 (May 1984): 323–327.

Comer, James P. "New Haven's School Community Connection." *Educational Leadership* 44 (March 1987): 13–16.

Comer, James P., and Norris M. Haynes, Muriel Hamilton-Lee, James Boger, and David Pollock. "Academic and Affective Gains from the School Development Program: A Model for School Improvement." Paper presented at the annual meeting of the American Psychological Association, Washington, DC, August 1986.

Commins, Nancy L., and Ofelia B. Miramontes. "Perceived and Actual Linguistic Competence: A Descriptive Study of Four Low-Achieving Hispanic Bilingual Students." *American Educational Research Journal* 26 (Winter 1989): 443–472.

Cooper, Laura A. "The Effective Schools Literature as a Basis for School Improvement Efforts." Ed.D. qualifying paper, Harvard Graduate School of Education, 1984.

Courts, George Roger. "An Investigation of Student Teachers' Acquisition of Specific Teaching Behaviors Modeled by Cooperating Teachers." Ed.D. diss., University of Cincinnati, 1983.

Crawford, George J., Cecil Miskel, and M. Claradine Johnson. "An Urban School Renewal Program: A Case Analysis." *The Urban Review* 12 (4): 175–198.

Cremin, Lawrence A. "The Free School Movement—A Perspective." *Today's Education* 63 (September 1974): 71–74.

Cremin, Lawrence A. *The Education of the Educating Professions.* Washington, DC: American Association of Colleges for Teacher Education, 1977.

Cremin, Lawrence A. *American Education: The Metropolitan Experience, 1875–1980.* New York: Harper & Row, 1988.

Crockett, Walter H., and others. "Report on TTT Site Visits Conducted in November and December, 1969: An Overview." Clearinghouse on Teacher Education. ERIC Document Reproduction Service No. ED 043 597.

Cuban, Larry. "Teacher and Community." *Harvard Educational Review* 39 (Spring 1969): 253–272.

Cuban, Larry. *To Make a Difference. Teaching in the Inner City.* New York: Free Press, 1970.

Cuban, Larry. "Persistence of the Inevitable. The Teacher-Centered Classroom." *Education and Urban Society* 15 (November 1982): 26–41.

Cuban, Larry. "Effective Schools: A Friendly but Cautionary Note." *Phi Delta Kappan* 64 (June 1983): 695–702.

Cuban, Larry. *Constancy and Change in American Classrooms 1850–1980.* New York: Longman, 1984.

Cuban, Larry. "The Holmes Group Report: Why Reach Exceeds Grasp." *Teachers College Record* 88 (Spring 1987): 348–353.

Cusick, Philip. "Finding Meaning in Teaching: Teachers' Vision of Their School." *Education and Urban Society* 17 (May 1985): 355–364.

D'Amico, Joseph. "Each Effective School May Be One of a Kind." *Educational Leadership* 40 (December 1982): 61–62.

Darling-Hammond, Linda, and Barnett Berry. *The Evolution of Teacher Policy.* Santa Monica, CA: Rand Corp., 1988.

Darling-Hammond, Linda and other. "Career Choices for Minorities: Who Will Teach?" Paper prepared for the National Education Association and Council of Chief State School Offices Task Force on Minorities in Teaching, June 1987.

Davidson, Edmonia W. "Education and Black Cities: Demographic Background." *The Journal of Negro Education* 42 (Summer 1973): 233–260.

Davies, Don, ed. *Communities and Their Schools.* New York: McGraw Hill, 1981.

Davies, Don. "Looking for an Ecological Solution: Planning to Improve the Education of Disadvantaged Children." *Equity and Choice* 4 (Fall 1987): 3–7.

Delpit, Lisa D. "Skills and Other Dilemmas of a Progressive Black Educator." *Harvard Educational Review* 56 (November 1986): 379–385.

Delpit, Lisa D. "The Silenced Dialogue." *Harvard Educational Review* 58 (August 1988): 280–298.

Deutsch, Martin. "The Role of Social Class in Language Development." In *Education of the Disadvantaged,* edited by Harry A. Passow, Miriam Goldberg, and Abraham J. Tannenbaum. New York: Holt, Rinehart & Winston, 1967.

Dewey, John. "The Relation of Theory to Practice in Education." In *Third Yearbook,* Part I. Chicago: National Society for the Scientific Study of Education, 1904.

DeYoung, Alan J. "Educational Excellence Versus Teacher Professionalism: Towards Some Conceptual Clarity." *The Urban Review* 18 (1986): 71–84.

DiLeonardo, Micaela. "Who's Really Getting Paid?" *The Nation* 14 (May 1990): 672–675.

Dodson, Dan. "Education and the Powerless." In *Education of the Disadvantaged,* edited by Harry A. Passow, Miriam Goldberg, and Abraham J. Tannenbaum. New York: Holt, Rinehart & Winston, 1967.

Dow, Gwyneth. *Learning to Teach: Teaching to Learn.* Boston: Routledge & Kegan Paul, 1979.

Downing, Gertrude, Robert W. Edgar, Albert J. Harris, Leonard Kornberg, and Helen F. Storen. *The Preparation of Teachers for Schools in Culturally Deprived Neighborhoods*. Flushing: The BRIDGE Project, City University of New York, Queens College, 1965.

Draper, Hal. *Karl Marx's Theory of Revolution*. Vols. 1–4. New York: Monthly Review Press, 1990.

Draper, Hal. "The Two Souls of Socialism." *New Politics*, N.S. 3 (Summer 1990): 129–156.

Dreeben, Robert. "Comments on *Tomorrow's Teachers*." *Teachers College Record* 88 (Spring 1987): 359–365.

Drucker, Ernest. "Cognitive Styles and Class Stereotypes." In *The Culture of Poverty: A Critique*, edited by Eleanor Leacock. New York: Simon & Schuster, 1971.

Dunne, Faith Weinstein. Review of *Don't Smile Until Christmas*, by Kevin Ryan. *Harvard Educational Review* 41 (August 1971): 401–408.

Dunne, Faith Weinstein. "Survival of the Innovative Teacher: Preparing Liberal Arts Graduates to Work for Change in the Public Schools." Ed.D. diss., Harvard Graduate School of Education, 1973.

Dworkin, Martin, ed. *Dewey on Education*. New York: Teachers College Press, 1959.

Eastman, George H. "John Dewey's Ideas on Teacher Education: The Chicago Years 1894–1904." Ed.D. qualifying paper, Harvard Graduate School of Education, 1963.

Edelfelt, Roy A., Ronald Corwin, and Elizabeth Hanna. *Lessons from the Teacher Corps*. Washington, DC: National Education Association, 1974. ERIC Document Reproduction Service No. ED 099 382.

Edmonds, Ronald. "A Theory and Design of Social Service Reform." *Social Policy* 15 (Fall 1984): 57–64.

Eisenberg, Leon. "Strengths of the Inner City Child." In *Education of the Disadvantaged*, edited by Harry A. Passow, Miriam Goldberg, and Abraham J. Tannenbaum. New York: Holt, Rinehart & Winston, 1967.

Elisberg, Joan Sered. "A Study of Selected Master of Arts in Teaching Programs in the United States." Ph.D. diss., Northwestern University, 1981.

Elliott, Peggy G., and Robert E. Mays. *Early Field Experiences in Teacher Education*. Bloomington, IN: Phi Delta Kappa Educational Foundation, 1979.

Epps, Edgar G. "Improving the Effectiveness of Urban Schools: Instruction." In *1978 Urban Conference Report*, edited by Marvin J. Fruth and Booker Gardner. Madison: Wisconsin Research and Development Center for Individualized Schooling, 1979. ERIC Document Reproduction Service No. ED 185 218.

Fillmore, Lily Wong, and Concepcion Valdez. "Teaching Bilingual Learners." In *Handbook of Research in Teaching*, edited by Merlin C. Wittrock. New York: Macmillan, 1986.

Fine, Michelle. "Why Urban Adolescents Drop Into and Out of Public High School." *Teachers College Record* 87 (Spring 1986): 393–409.

Fine, Michelle. *Framing Dropouts: Notes on the Politics of an Urban High School*. Albany: State University of New York Press, 1991.

Finkelstein, Barbara. "Education and the Retreat from Democracy in the United States, 1979–198?" *Teachers College Record* 86 (Winter 1984): 275–282.

Fisher, Maxine P. "Creating Ethnic Identity: Asian Indians in the New York City Area." *Urban Anthropology* 7 (Fall 1978): 271–285.

Fordham, Signithia, and John U. Ogbu. "Black Students' School Success: Coping with the Burden of 'Acting White.'" *The Urban Review* 18 (Fall 1986): 176–206.

Freire, Paulo. *Pedagogy of the Oppressed.* New York: Continuum, 1982.

Furno, Orlando F., and J. S. Kidd. *New Teachers for the Inner City.* Washington, DC: Capitol Publications, 1974.

Gage, N. L. *Teacher Effectiveness and Teacher Education.* Palo Alto, CA: Pacific Books, 1972.

Galambos, Eva C., ed. *Improving Teacher Education.* San Francisco: Jossey-Bass, 1986.

Gilbert, Shirl E. II, and Geneva Gay. "Improving the Success in School of Poor Black Children." *Phi Delta Kappan* 67 (October 1985): 133–137.

Ginsberg, Rick, Henrietta Schwartz, George Olson, and Albert Bennett. "Working Conditions in Urban Schools." *The Urban Review* 19 (Spring 1986): 3–23.

Giroux, Henry A., and Peter McLaren. "Teacher Education and the Politics of Engagement: The Case for Democratic Schooling." *Harvard Educational Review* 56 (August 1986): 213–238.

Giroux, Henry A., Anthony N. Penna, and William F. Pinar, eds. *Curriculum and Instruction: Alternatives in Education.* Berkeley, CA: McCutchan, 1981.

Gittell, Marilyn, with B. Hoffacker, Eleanor Rollins, and Samuel Foster. *Citizen Organizations: Citizen Participation in Educational Decisionmaking.* N.p. Contract No. 400-76-0115. Institute for Responsive Education/NIE, July 1979.

Glasser, Ira. "The Burden of Blame: A Report on the Ocean Hill–Brownsville School Controversy." *Urban Education* 4 (Summer 1969): 7–24.

Glazer, Nathan. "The Schools of the Minor Professions." *Minerva* 12 (July 1974): 346–364.

Gold, Milton J. "Programs for the Disadvantaged at Hunter College." *Phi Delta Kappan* 48 (March 1967): 365.

Gold, Milton J. "Community Participation in Teacher Education: A TTT Innovation. A Survey of Community Participation in Selected TTT Projects." City University of New York, Hunter College, 1971. ERIC Document Reproduction Service No. ED 056 984.

Gold, Milton J. "Hunter College TTT Program: Training the Teachers of Teachers Elementary Education." City University of New York, Hunter College, 1972. ERIC Document Reproduction Service No. ED 075 433.

Goldberg, Miriam. "Factors Affecting Educational Attainment in Depressed Urban Areas." In *Education of the Disadvantaged,* edited by Harry A. Passow, Miriam Goldberg, and Abraham J. Tannenbaum. New York: Holt, Rinehart & Winston, 1967.

Goldenberg, Claude, and Ronald Gallimore. "Local Knowledge and Educational Change: A Case Study of Early Spanish Reading Improvement." *Educational Researcher* 20 (November 1991): 2–14.

Goldsmith, Clarence Hayden. "An Investigation of the Relationship between Selected Teacher Characteristics and the Effectiveness of Teachers of Culturally Disadvantaged and Non-Disadvantaged Elementary School Students." Ph.D. diss., St. Louis University, 1970.

Gollnick, Donna M., Kobla I. M. Osayande, and Jack Levy. *Multicultural Teacher Education*. Washington, DC: American Association of Colleges for Teacher Education, 1980.

Good, Thomas L., and Jere E. Brophy. "School Effects." In *Handbook of Research in Teaching*, edited by Merlin C. Wittrock. New York: Macmillan, 1986.

Goodenow, Ronald K., and Diane Ravitch, eds. *Schools in Cities*. New York: Holmes & Meier, 1983.

Goodman, David. *Delivering Educational Service: Urban Schools and Schooling Policy*. New York: Teachers College Press, 1977.

Goodman, Paul. "The Universal Trap." In *The Urban School Crisis*, edited by League for Industrial Democracy and United Federation of Teachers. New York: League for Industrial Democracy and United Federation of Teachers, 1966.

Gordon, Beverly M. "Teaching Teachers: *Nation at Risk* and the Issue of Knowledge in Teacher Education." *The Urban Review* 17 (Spring 1985): 33–46.

Grace, Gerald, ed. *Education and the City*. Boston: Routledge & Kegan Paul, 1984.

Graff, Harvey J. *The Labyrinth of Literacy*. New York: Falmer Press, 1987.

Graham, Patricia Albjerg. "Schools: Cacophony about Practice, Silence about Purpose." *Daedalus* 113 (Fall 1984): 29–58.

Graham, Patricia Albjerg. "Black Teachers: A Drastically Scarce Resource." *Phi Delta Kappan* 68 (April 1987): 598–605.

Grant, Carl A. "Education That's Multicultural for Urban Schools: Rationale and Recommendation." In *1978 Urban Conference Report*, edited by Marvin J. Fruth and Booker Gardner. Madison: Wisconsin Research and Development Center for Individualized Schooling, 1979. ERIC Document Reproduction Service No. ED 185 218.

Grant, Carl A., ed. *Preparing for Reflective Teaching*. Boston: Allyn & Bacon, Inc., 1984.

Grant, Carl A. "Urban Teachers: Their New Colleagues and Curriculum." *Phi Delta Kappan* 70 (June 1989): 764–770.

Grant, Gerald. *The World We Created at Hamilton High*. Cambridge, MA: Harvard Univ. Press, 1988.

Greene, Maxine. "Review of *Changing Education* and *This Magazine Is about Schools.*" *Harvard Educational Review* 37 (Fall 1967): 670–673.

Grotelueschen, Arden D., and Gary A. Storm. "The National TTT Program: Noteworthy Activities and Outcomes. Evaluation No. 3." Urbana: Illinois Univ., 1970. ERIC Document Reproduction Service No. ED 052 146.

Guerrero, Guadalupe E. "Teacher Role Conflicts in Urban Schools: A Review of the Literature." Ed.D. qualifying paper, Harvard Graduate School of Education, 1977.

Guthrie, James W. "Education R & D's Lament (and What to Do About It)." *Educational Researcher* 19 (March 1990): 26–34.

Gutmann, Amy. *Democratic Education.* Princeton, NJ: Princeton Univ. Press, 1987.

Haberman, Martin. "Recruiting and Selecting Teachers for Urban Schools." November 1987. ERIC Document Reproduction Service No. ED 292 942.

Haberman, Martin. *Preparing Teachers for Urban Schools.* Bloomington, IN: Phi Delta Kappa Educational Foundation, 1988.

Harste, Jerome C., and others. "Some Recommendations to Federal Agency Personnel Regarding the Evaluation of Education." Teacher Education Forum Series, Vol. 2., No. 8. Bloomington: Indiana Univ., 1974. ERIC Document Reproduction Service No. ED 099 318.

Harvard Educational Review. *Perspectives on Inequality.* Reprint Series No. 8. Vol. 43 (February 1973).

Haubrich, Vernon F. "Federal Funds and Teacher Education." 1966, ERIC Document Reproduction Service No. ED 012 699.

Hawley, William B., and Joseph T. Vallanti. "Trainers of Teachers of Teachers." U.S. Office of Education Contract No. OEG 0-9-324146-2165-721. East Lansing: Michigan State University, 1970. ERIC Document Reproduction Service No. ED 043 593.

Hawley, Willis D., and Susan J. Rosenholtz. *Achieving Quality Integrated Education.* Washington, DC: National Education Association, 1986.

Heath, Shirley Brice. *Ways with Words.* New York: Cambridge Univ. Press, 1983.

Hein, George E. "The Social History of Open Education: Austrian and Soviet Schools in the 1920's." *The Urban Review* 8 (Summer 1975): 96–119.

Hernandez, Norma G. "Multicultural Education and CBTE: A Vehicle for Reform." Paper presented. N.p., 1974. ERIC Document Reproduction Service No. ED 091 386.

Hilbert, Richard A. "CBTE Versus the Real World." *Urban Education* 16 (January 1982): 379–398.

Hilliard, Asa G. "Restructuring Teacher Education for Multicultural Imperatives." In *Multicultural Education Through Competency Based Teacher Education,* edited by William A. Hunt. Washington, DC: American Association of Colleges for Teacher Education, 1974.

Hite, Herbert F., and William H. Drummond. "The Teacher Corps and Collaboration." *Journal of Teacher Education* 26 (Summer 1975): 133–134.

Hodgkinson, Harold L. *All One System.* Washington, DC: Institute for Educational Leadership, 1985.

The Holmes Group. *Tomorrow's Teachers: A Report of the Holmes Group.* East Lansing, MI: The Holmes Group, 1986.

The Holmes Group. *The Holmes Group Forum* 4 (Fall 1989).

Holmes, Steven A. "Senate Votes Bush Education Bill, with Plan for Teacher Standards." *New York Times,* 8 February 1990, p. 26.

Holt, John. *The Underachieving School.* New York: Putnam, 1969.

Holusha, John. "Are We Eating Our Seed Corn?" *New York Times*, 13 May 1990, section 3, p. 1.

Hooper, Susan. *Good Teachers: An Unblinking Look at Supply and Preparedness.* N.p., National School Boards Association, 1987.

Houston, James E., ed. *Thesaurus of ERIC Descriptors*, 11th ed. Phoenix, AZ: Oryx Press, 1987.

Houston, Robert W., and Robert B. Howsam, eds. *Competency-Based Teacher Education: Progress, Problems, and Prospects.* Chicago: Science Research Associates, 1972.

Howe, Harold II. "Education Moves to Center State: An Overview of Recent Studies." *Phi Delta Kappan* 65 (November 1983): 167–172.

Howe, Harold II. "Introduction to Symposium on the Year of the Reports: Responses from the Educational Community." *Harvard Educational Review* 54 (February 1984): 1–5.

Hunt, J. McVicker. *The Challenge of Incompetence and Poverty.* Urbana: Univ. of Illinois Press, 1969.

Hunt, William A., ed. *Multicultural Education Through Competency Based Teacher Education.* Washington, DC: American Association of Colleges for Teacher Education, 1974.

Jencks, Christopher. "Inequality in Retrospect." *Harvard Educational Review* 43 (February 1973), Reprint Series #8.

Jencks, Christopher, Marshall Smith, Henry Acland, Mary Jo Bane, David Cohen, Herbert Gintis, Barbara Heyns, and Stephen Michelson. *Inequality.* New York: Harper & Row, 1972.

Johnson, Susan Moore. "Schoolwork and Its Reform." In *The Politics of Reforming School Administration*, edited by Jane Hannaway and Robert Crowsor. New York: Falmer Press, 1989.

Joint Center for Political Studies. *Visions of a Better Way: A Black Appraisal of Public Schooling.* Washington, DC: Joint Center for Political Studies Press, 1989.

Joselow, Froma. "What's New in the Costume Jewelry Business." *New York Times*, 16 April 1989, section F, p. 17.

Journal of Teacher Education 26 (Summer 1975): 112–118. "The Teacher Corps Concept: A *Journal* Interview [with Richard Graham]."

Kaestle, Carl. *The Evolution of an Urban School System: New York City 1750–1850.* Cambridge, MA: Harvard Univ. Press, 1973.

Kantor, Harvey, and Robert Lowe. Review of *How Teachers Taught* by Larry Cuban. *Harvard Educational Review* 56 (February 1986): 69–76.

Katz, Michael B., ed. *School Reform: Past and Present.* Boston: Little, Brown, 1971.

Katz, Michael B. *Reconstructing American Education.* Cambridge, MA: Harvard Univ. Press, 1987.

Katznelson, Ira, and Margaret Weir. *Schooling for All: Class, Race and the Decline of the Democratic Ideal.* New York: Basic Books, 1985.

Kazemak, Francis E. "Necessary Changes." *Harvard Educational Review* 58 (November 1988): 464–487.

Kearns, David. "Competitiveness Begins at School." *New York Times,* 17 December 1989, section 3, p. 2.

Kegan, Robert. *The Evolving Self.* Cambridge, MA: Harvard Univ. Press, 1982.

Kelman, Peter Helmut. "Needs Assessment for the Design of an Urban Master of Arts in Teaching Program." Ed.D. diss., Harvard Graduate School of Education, 1974.

Kemble, Eugenia, and Bernard McKenna. *PBTE: Viewpoints of Two Teacher Organizations.* Washington, DC: American Association of Colleges for Teacher Education, 1975.

Kennedy, Mary M. "Kenneth Zeichner Reflecting on Reflection." *National Center for Research on Teacher Education Colloquy* 2 (Spring 1989): 15–21.

Kennedy, Mary M. "An Agenda for Research on Teacher Learning." *National Center for Research on Teacher Learning* (Spring 1991).

Kennedy, Mary M. "Some Surprising Findings on How Teachers Learn to Teach." *Educational Leadership* 49 (November 1991): 14–17.

Kerr, Donna H. "Teaching Competence and Teacher Education in the United States." *Teachers College Record* 84 (Spring 1983): 525–552.

Kirp, David L. "Introduction: The Fourth R: Reading, Writing, Rithmetic — and Rules." In *School Days, Rule Days,* edited by David L. Kirp and Donald N. Jensen. Philadelphia: Falmer Press, 1986.

Kirp, David L., and Donald N. Jensen, eds. *School Days, Rule Days.* Philadelphia: Falmer Press, 1986.

Kiss, Stephen Howard. "The Influence of Content Area, School Location, and Cooperating Teacher on Change in the Pupil Control Ideology of Secondary-Level Student Teachers." Ph.D. diss., New York University, 1981.

Kohl, Herbert. *Half the House.* New York: Dutton, 1974.

Kohl, Herbert. *On Teaching.* New York: Schocken Books, 1976.

Kreuter, Mortimer. "The Teacher in the Brown Paper Bag." *The Urban Review* 1 (May 1966).

Labaree, David F. "Power, Knowledge, and the Rationalization of Teaching: A Genealogy of the Movement to Professionalize Teaching." *Harvard Educational Review* 62 (Summer 1992): 123–154.

Lanier, Judith E., and Judith W. Little. "Research on Teacher Education." In *Handbook of Research in Teacher Education,* edited by Merlin C. Wittrock. New York: Macmillan, 1986.

Larner, Jeremy. "The New York School Crisis." In *The Urban School Crisis,* edited by League for Industrial Development and United Federation of Teachers. New York: League for Industrial Development and United Federation of Teachers, 1966.

Lawn, Martin, and Gerald Grace, eds. *Teachers: The Culture and Politics of Work.* Philadelphia: Falmer Press, 1987.

Leacock, Eleanor, ed. *The Culture of Poverty: A Critique.* New York: Simon & Schuster, 1971.

League for Industrial Democracy and United Federation of Teachers. *The Urban School Crisis.* New York: League for Industrial Democracy and United Federation of Teachers, 1966.

Lenin, V. I. *Collected Works*, 28, 29, 33, 36, 44, 45. London: Lawrence & Wishart edition of Progress Publishers, Moscow, 1965.

Leslie, Larry L., Joel R. Levin, and David R. Wampler. "The Effect of Preservice Experience with the Disadvantaged on First-Year Teachers in Disadvantaged Schools." *Education and Urban Society* 3 (August 1971): 398–413.

Levin, Henry M. *Educational Reform for Disadvantaged Students: An Emerging Crisis*. Washington, DC: National Education Association, 1986.

Levin, Henry M. "Mapping the Economics of Education." *Educational Researcher* 18 (May 1989) 13–16.

Levine, Murray, and Adeline Levine. *A Social History of Helping Services*. New York: Appleton Century Crofts, 1970.

Lieberman, Myron. "Are Teachers Underpaid?" *The Public Interest* 84 (Summer 1986): 12–28.

Linton, Thomas E., and Jack L. Nelson. "Teacher Education: Are We Blind to Urban Problems?" *The Urban Review* 2 (Summer 1979): 55–62.

Lipow, Arthur. *Authoritarian Socialism in America: Edward Bellamy and the Nationalist Movement*. Berkeley, CA: Univ. of California Press, 1983.

Lipsky, Michael. *Street-Level Bureaucracy*. New York: Russell Sage Foundation, 1980.

Liston, Daniel P., and Kenneth M. Zeichner. "Critical Pedagogy and Teacher Education." *Journal of Education* 169 (1987): 117–143.

Liston, Daniel P., and Kenneth M. Zeichner. *Teacher Education and the Social Context of Schooling*. Paper presented at the annual convention of the American Educational Research Association, Boston, April 1990.

Liston, Daniel P., and Zeichner, Kenneth M. *Teacher Education and the Social Conditions of Schooling*. New York: Routledge, 1991.

Little, Judith Warren. "Teachers As Colleagues." In *Educators' Handbook: A Research Perspective*, edited by V. Richardson-Koehler. New York: Longman, 1987.

Lomotey, Kofi, and Austin D. Swanson. "Urban and Rural Schools Research: Implications for School Governance." *Education and Urban Society* 21 (August 1989): 436–454.

Lortie, Dan. "Observations on Teaching as Work." In *Second Handbook of Research on Teaching*, edited by Robert M. W. Travers. Chicago: Rand McNally, 1973.

Lortie, Dan. *Schoolteacher*. Chicago: Univ. of Chicago Press, 1975.

Lowe, Robert, and Harvey Kantor. "Considerations on Writing the History of Educational Reform in the 1960's." *Educational Theory* 39 (Winter 1989): 1–9.

McCullough, Tom. "Urban Education — 'It's No Big Thing.'" *Urban Education* 9 (July 1974): 117–135.

McDiarmid, G. Williamson. "What To Do about Differences? A Study of Multicultural Education for Teacher Trainees in the Los Angeles Unified School District." *Journal of Teacher Education* 43 (March–April 1992): 83–93.

Manny, Frank. *City Training Schools for Teachers.* Washington, DC: U.S. Bureau of Education, Bulletin No. 47, 1915.

Mark, Jonathan H., and Barry D. Anderson. "Schools and the Transformation of the Metropolis." *The Urban Review* 16 (1984): 3–23.

Marsh, David. "An Evaluation of Sixth Cycle Teacher Corps Graduates." *Journal of Teacher Education* 26 (Summer 1975): 139–140.

Medley, Donald M., Robert S. Soar, and Ruth Soar. *Assessment and Research in Teacher Education: Focus on PBTE.* Washington, DC: American Association of Colleges for Teacher Education, 1975.

Menand, Louis. "The Hammer and the Nail." *The New Yorker* (July 20, 1992): 79–84.

Metz, Mary Haywood. *Classrooms and Corridors: The Crisis of Authority in Desegregated Secondary Schools.* Berkeley: Univ. of California Press, 1978.

Miller, Lamar P. "Improving the Effectiveness of Urban Schools: Teacher Education." In *1978 Urban Conference Report,* edited by Marvin J. Fruth and Booker Gardner. Madison: Wisconsin Research and Development Center for Individualized Schooling, 1979. ERIC Document Reproduction Service No. ED 185 218.

Morgan, Edward P. "Effective Teaching in the Urban High School." *Urban Education* 14 (July 1979): 161–181.

Murnane, Richard. "Education and the Productivity of the Workforce: Looking Ahead." In *American Living Standards,* edited by Robert Z. Lawrence, Robert E. Litan, and Charles L. Schultze. Washington, DC: Brookings Institution, 1992.

National Advisory Council on Education Professions Development. *Competency Based Teacher Education: Toward a Consensus.* Washington, DC: National Advisory Council on Education Professions Development, 1976.

National Advisory Council on Education Professions Development. "Teacher Corps: Past or Prologue?" Washington DC: National Advisory Council on Education Professions Development, July 1975. ERIC Document Reproduction Service No. ED 109 083.

National Coalition of Advocates for Students. *Barriers to Excellence: Our Children at Risk.* Boston: National Coalition of Advocates for Students, 1986.

National Commission for Excellence in Teacher Education. *A Call for Change in Teacher Education.* Washington, DC: American Association of Colleges for Teacher Education, 1985.

National Commission on Excellence in Education. *A Nation at Risk.* Washington, DC: U.S. Department of Education, 1983.

National Council of Teachers of English. *A Statement on the Preparation of Teachers of English and the Language Arts.* Urbana, IL: National Council of Teachers of English, 1976.

National Education Association. *Excellence in Our Schools: Teacher Education, an Action Plan.* Washington, DC: National Education Association, 1982.

National Research Council. *Toward Understanding Teacher Supply and De-*

mand: Priorities for Research and Development. New York: National Academy Press, 1988.

Nelson, Gaylord. Guest editorial in *Journal of Teacher Education* 26 (Summer 1975): 98–99.

Needham, Charles C. "The Effect of Intern-Teaching in Schools Serving Disadvantaged Students on Attitudes of Intern-Teachers Toward Disadvantaged Students." Ed.D. diss., University of Tulsa, 1973.

Newmann, Fred. "Desoto High School." In *Portraits of High Schools*, edited by Vito Perrone and associates. Princeton, NJ: Princeton Univ. Press, 1985.

Nickse, Ruth S. "How to Change the Schools from Inside: Teachers as Change Agents." 1973. ERIC Document Reproduction Service No. ED 084 224.

Oakes, Jeannie. "The Reproduction of Inequity: The Content of Secondary School Tracking." *The Urban Review* 14 (Summer 1982): 107–120.

O'Brian, John L. "A Master's Degree Program for the Preparation of Teachers of Disadvantaged Youth." In *Preparing to Teach the Disadvantaged*, edited by Bruce W. Tuckman and John L. O'Brian. New York: Free Press, 1969.

Odden, Allan. "Financing Educational Excellence." *Phi Delta Kappan* 65 (January 1984): 311–318.

Ogbu, John U. "The Individual in Collective Adaptation: A Framework for Focusing on Academic Underperformance and Dropping Out Among Involuntary Minorities." In *Dropouts from School: Issues, Dilemmas, and Solutions*, edited by Lois Weis, Eleanor Farrar, and Hugh G. Petrie. Albany: State Univ. of New York Press, 1989.

Ogletree, Earl J., and Malvern L. Ore, eds. *Urban Education: Perspectives and Issues.* Washington, DC: Univ. Press of America, 1977.

Ornstein, Allan C. *Educating the Inner City Child: A Review of Research Findings in Two Decades.* Chicago: Center for Urban Policy at Loyola Univ. of Chicago, 1981.

Ornstein, Allan C., and Harriet Talmage. "A Dissenting View on Accountability." *Urban Education* 8 (July 1973): 133–152.

Ornstein, Allan C., and Harriet Talmage. "Teachers' Perceptions of Decision Making Roles and Responsibilities in Defining Accountability." *Journal of Negro Education* 42 (Spring 1973): 212–221.

Otten, Jane, ed. *An Experiment in Planned Change.* Washington, DC: American Association of State Colleges and Universities, 1973.

Paley, Vivian Gussin. *White Teacher.* Cambridge, MA: Harvard Univ. Press, 1979.

Parker, John L. "Staffing Schools for the Urban Disadvantaged." Ed.D. diss., Harvard Graduate School of Education, 1968.

Passow, Harry A., Miriam Goldberg, and Abraham J. Tannenbaum, eds. *Education of the Disadvantaged.* New York: Holt, Rinehart & Winston, 1967.

Payne, Charles M. *Getting What We Ask For: The Ambiguity of Success and Failure in Urban Education.* Westport, CT: Greenwood Press, 1984.

Perrone, Vito. "Parents as Partners." *The Urban Review* 5 (November 1971): 35–40.

Perrone, Vito. "Observation on the Carnegie Themes." In *Portraits of High Schools*, edited by Vito Perrone and associates. Princeton, NJ: Princeton Univ. Press, 1985.

Perrone, Vito and associates. *Portraits of High Schools*. Princeton, NJ: Princeton Univ. Press, 1985.

Piccigallo, Philip R. "Renovating Urban Schools Is Fundamental to Improving Them." *Phi Delta Kappan* 70 (January 1989): 402–406.

Posner, George J. *Field Experience: A Guide to Reflective Teaching*. New York: Longman, 1985.

Powell, Arthur G. *The Uncertain Profession: Harvard and the Search for Educational Authority*. Cambridge, MA: Harvard Univ. Press, 1980.

Powell, Arthur G., Eleanor Farrar, and David K. Cohen. *Shopping Mall High School*. Boston: Houghton Mifflin, 1985.

Prakash, Madhu Suri. "Reforming the Teaching of Teachers: Trends, Contradictions, and Challenges." *Teachers College Record* 88 (Winter 1986): 217–240.

Quality Education for Minorities Project. Unpublished testimony from regional meetings of the Quality Education for Minorities Project. Washington, DC: Quality Education for Minorities Project.

Quality Education for Minorities Project. *Education that Works: An Action Plan for the Education of Minorities*. Washington, DC: Quality Education for Minorities Project, 1990.

Ralph, John. "Improving Education for the Disadvantaged: Do We Know Whom to Help?" *Phi Delta Kappan* 70 (January 1989): 395–401.

Ralph, John H., and James Fennessey. "Science or Reform: Some Questions about the Effective Schools Model." *Phi Delta Kappan* 64 (June 1983): 689–694.

Ravitch, Diane. "Programs, Placebos, Panaceas." *The Urban Review* 2 (April 1968): 8–11.

Ravitch, Diane. *The Great School Wars, New York City 1805–1973*. New York: Basic Books, 1974.

Ravitch, Diane. *The Revisionists Revised*. New York: Basic Books, 1977.

Ravitch, Diane, and Ronald K. Goodenow, eds. *Educating an Urban People*. New York: Teachers College Press, 1981.

Ravitch, Diane. *The Troubled Crusade: American Education 1945–1980*. New York: Basic Books, 1983.

Raywid, Mary Anne. "Tomorrow's Teachers and Today's Schools." *Teachers College Record* 88 (Spring 1987): 411–418.

Riessman, Frank. *The Culturally Deprived Child*. New York: Harper & Row, 1962.

Riessman, Frank. *The Inner City Child*. New York: Harper & Row, 1976.

Rist, Ray C. *The Urban School: A Factory for Failure*. Cambridge, MA: M.I.T. Press, 1973.

Rittenmeyer, Dennis C., and James R. K. Heinen. "The Preparation of Urban Educators: A Survey of Urban School Systems." Paper presented to the second annual Urban Education Conference, Milwaukee, November 1977. ERIC Document Reproduction Service No. ED 146 283.

Rivlin, Harry N. "A Case Study in Changing the Governance of a Teacher Education Program." ERIC Document Reproduction Service No. ED 091 349.

Roberts, Joan I. *Scene of the Battle.* Garden City, NY: Doubleday, 1970.

Rogers, David. *110 Livingston Street: Politics and Bureaucracy in the New York City Schools.* New York: Random House, 1968.

Rosenbaum, James E., Marilyn J. Kulieke, and Leonard S. Rubinowitz. "White Suburban Schools' Responses to Low-Income Black Children: Sources of Successes and Problems." *The Urban Review* 20 (Spring 1988): 28–31.

Rossmiller, Richard A. "Financing Urban Schools." In *1978 Urban Conference Report,* edited by Marvin J. Fruth and Booker Gardner. Madison: Wisconsin Research and Development Center for Individualized Schooling, 1979. ERIC Document Reproduction Service No. ED 185 218.

Roth, Robert A. "PBTE Certification: A Survey of the States." New Jersey State Education Department, December 1972. ERIC Document Reproduction Service No. ED 070 753.

Roth, Robert A. *Teaching and Teacher Education: Implementing Reform.* Bloomington, IN: Phi Delta Kappa Educational Foundation, 1986.

Sales, Joseph, Sr. "Teacher Attitudes Toward the Disadvantaged: A Longitudinal Comparison of Composite Models of Strongest and Weakest Participants in Elementary Education Training Program for Central-City Detroit." Ed.D. diss., Wayne State Univ., 1971.

Saltzman, Harold. *Race War in High School.* New Rochelle, NY: Arlington House, 1972.

Sandefur, Walter S., and Willis L. Nicklas. "Competency-Based Teacher Education in AACTE Institutions: An Update." *Phi Delta Kappan* 62 (June 1981): 747–748.

Sandholtz, Judy Haymore. "The Subject Matters More Than We Thought." Paper presented at the annual convention of the American Educational Research Association, Boston, April 1990.

Sarason, Seymour B. *The Culture of the School and the Problem of Change.* Boston: Allyn & Bacon, 1971.

Sarason, Seymour B., Kenneth S. Davidson, and Burton Blatt. *The Preparation of Teachers: An Unstudied Problem in Education.* 2d ed. Cambridge, MA: Brookline Books, 1986.

Schiff, Martin. "Community Control of Inner-City Schools and Education Achievement." *Urban Education* 10 (January 1976): 415–432.

Schneider, Barbara. "Assuring Educational Quality for Children At Risk." Paper presented at the annual convention of the American Educational Research Association, Boston, April 1990.

Schwartz, Judah L. "Assessment that Respects Complexity in Individuals and Programs." Paper prepared for the National Conference on Urban Education, St. Louis, July 1978. ERIC Document Reproduction Service No. ED 185 159.

Sedlak, Maurice, and Steven Schlossman. *Who Will Teach? Historical Perspec-*

tives on the Changing Appeal of Teaching as a Profession. Santa Monica, CA: Rand Corp., 1986.

Seeley, David S. "Education Through Partnership." *Educational Leadership* 40 (November 1982): 42–43.

Seeley, David S. "Educational Partnerships and the Dilemmas of School Reform." *Phi Delta Kappan* 65 (February 1984): 383–388.

Shanker, Albert. "The Real Meaning of the New York City Teachers Strike." *Phi Delta Kappan* 50 (April 1969): 434–442.

Shanker, Albert. "Meeting Education's Challenges — Teacher Unionists Prepare for Action." *Report on the State of the Union, 1976–77.* Washington, DC: American Federation of Teachers, 1977.

Shanker, Albert. "The Making of a Profession." *American Educator* (Fall 1985): p. 10.

Sherman, Robert R., and Joseph Kirschner, eds. *Understanding History of Education.* 2d ed. Cambridge, MA: Schenkman, 1984.

Shor, Ira. "Equality Is Excellence: Transforming Teacher Education and the Learning Process." *Harvard Educational Review* 56 (November 1986): 406–426.

Shor, Ira. *Culture Wars. School and Society in the Conservative Restoration 1969–1984.* New York: Routledge & Kegan Paul, 1987.

Shulman, Lee S. "Knowledge and Teaching: Foundations of the New Reform." *Harvard Educational Review* 57 (February 1987): 1–22.

Sizer, Theodore R. *Horace's Compromise. The Dilemma of the American High School.* Boston: Houghton Mifflin, 1984.

Slavin, Robert E., and Nancy A. Madden. "What Works for Students At Risk: A Research Synthesis." *Educational Leadership* 46 (February 1989): 4–13.

Sleeter, Christine E., and Carl A. Grant. "Success for All Students." *Phi Delta Kappan* 68 (December 1986): 297–299.

Smith, B. Othanel, ed. *Research on Teacher Education: A Symposium.* Englewood Cliffs, NJ: Prentice-Hall, 1971

Smith, B. Othanel, and others. *Teachers for the Real World.* Washington, DC: American Association of Colleges for Teacher Education, 1969.

Smith, Carol Payne. "Preparing Teachers for the Disadvantaged: Development and Procedures of an Experimental Program." Ph.D. diss., Michigan State University, 1971.

Smith, Gerald R., Jerome C. Harste, James M. Mahan, James M. Clark, Robert McGinty, and Stanley S. Shuner. "Stirrings in Teacher Education." U.S. Office of Education Contract. Bloomington: Indiana University, 1974.

Smith, Mary Lee. "Put to the Test: The Effects of External Testing on Teachers." *Educational Researcher* 20 (June/July 1991): 8–11.

Spratlen, Thaddeus H. "Financing Inner City Schools: Policy Aspects of Economics, Political, and Racial Disparity." *Urban Education* 42 (Summer 1973): 283–307.

Spring, Joel. "Education and the SONY War." *Phi Delta Kappan* 65 (April 1984): 534–537.

Steffensen, James P. "Teacher Corps: A Nervous Decade of Educational Innovation." *Journal of Teacher Education* 25 (Summer 1975): 110–111.

Stephenson, Robert S., and Daniel U. Levine. "Are Effective or Meritorious
Schools Meretricious?" *The Urban Review* 19 (1987): 25–34.

Stern, David, and John Harter. "Public Schools and Teachers Unions in the
Political Economy of the 1970's." In *Communities and Their Schools*, edited by Don Davies. New York: McGraw Hill, 1981.

Stinnett, T. M., ed. *Unfinished Business of the Teaching Profession in the
1970's*. Bloomington, IN: Phi Delta Kappa, 1971. ERIC Document Reproduction Service No. ED 073 069.

Storen, Helen F. *The First Semester: Beginning Teachers in Urban Schools*.
New York: Project TRUE, Hunter College of the City University of New
York, 1964.

Strike, Kenneth A. Review of *Keeping Track: How Schools Structure Inequality* by Jeannie Oakes. *Teachers College Record* 87 (Spring 1987): 441–444.

Styskal, Richard A. "Political Science Methodology in Evaluation: Power, Professionalism, and Organizational Commitment in TTT." Paper presented
at the annual meeting of the American Educational Research Association,
Chicago, April 1974. ERIC Document Reproduction Service No. ED 100
843.

Suzuki, Bob. "Curriculum Transformation for Multicultural Education." *Education and Urban Society* 16 (May 1984): 294–319.

Swick, Kevin James. "An Investigation of an Experimental Urban Teacher
Preparation Program: Implications for Teacher Preparation." Ph.D. diss.,
University of Connecticut, 1970.

Sykes, Gary. "Policy Initiatives for Developing a Teaching Profession." *Elementary School Journal* 86 (March 1986): 365–367.

Tamashiro, Roy T. "Evaluating the Impact of New Priorities in Teacher Education." Paper presented at the annual meeting of the American Association of Colleges for Teacher Education, Houston, February 1982. ERIC
Document Reproduction Service No. ED 215 965.

Tarr, Elvira R. "Some Philosophical Issues in Competency-Based Teacher Education." Paper presented at the annual meeting of the American Educational Research Association, New Orleans, February 1973. ERIC Document Reproduction Service No. 076 667.

"The Teacher Corps Concept: A *Journal* Interview." Interview with Richard
Graham. *Journal of Teacher Education* 26 (Summer 1975): 112–118.

Tewel, Kenneth J. "The Best Child I Ever Had: Teacher Influence on the
Decision-Making of Three Urban High School Principals." *Urban Education* 23 (April 1988): 24–41.

Tewel, Kenneth J., and Sidney Trubowitz, "The Minority Group: Teacher:
An Endangered Species." *Urban Education* 22 (October 1987): 355–365.

Timar, Thomas B., and David L. Kirp. *Managing Educational Excellence*.
New York: Falmer Press, 1988.

Toch, Thomas. "The Dark Side of the Excellence Movement." *Phi Delta Kappan* 66 (November 1984): 173–176.

Tom, Alan R. *How Should Teachers Be Educated: An Assessment of the Reform Reports*. Bloomington, IN: Phi Delta Kappa Educational Foundation, 1987.

Trachtenberg, Paul L. "The Bleak Plight of the Urban Teacher." *The Urban Review* 6 (1973): 51–56.

Travers, Robert M. W., ed. *Second Handbook of Research on Teaching*. Chicago: Rand McNally, 1973.

Travers, Robert M. W. *Empirically Based Teacher Education*. Paper presented at the annual meeting of the Society of Professors of Education, Chicago, February 1974.

Tuckman, Bruce W., and John L. O'Brian. *Preparing to Teach the Disadvantaged*. New York: Free Press, 1969.

Tyack, David B. *The One Best System*. Cambridge, MA: Harvard Univ. Press, 1974.

Tyack, David, and Elisabeth Hansot. *Managers of Virtue*. New York: Basic Books, 1982.

University of Virginia Evaluation Research Center. *TTT Final Evaluation Report*. Charlottesville: University of Virginia, 1973a.

University of Virginia Evaluation Research Center. *TTT In-Depth Study: City University of New York*. Charlottesville: University of Virginia, 1973b.

The Urban Review 2 (February 1967). Editorial, "Questions of Authority."

The Urban Review 2 (May 1968): 15–34. "The Controversy over the More Effective Schools: A Special Supplement."

The Urban Review 3 (November 1968): 18–27. Interview with Albert Shanker.

The Urban Review 13 (Summer 1981): 193–196. "Reforming the Large Urban High School." ERIC/CUE Urban Education Research Information.

Verstegen, Deborah A., and David L. Clark. "The Diminution in Federal Expenditures for Education During the Reagan Administration." *Phi Delta Kappan* 70 (October 1988): 134–138.

Villegas, Ana Maria. "School Failure and Cultural Mismatch: Another View." *The Urban Review* 20 (Winter 1988): 253–265.

Walker, Gloria Pryor. Review of *Black English* by J. L. Dillard. *The Journal of Negro Education* 42 (Winter 1973): 99–101.

Warshaw, Mimi. "Schoolopoly: Not a Game of Chance." *The Urban Review* 17 (1985): 265–268.

Washington, Bennetta B. "Cardozo Project in Urban Teaching: A Pilot Project in Curriculum Development Utilizing Returned Peace Corps Volunteers in an Urban High School." January 1964. ERIC Document Reproduction Service No. ED 001 653.

Washington, DC, Public Schools. "The Urban Teacher Corps 1963–1968. Description and Philosophy." May 1968. ERIC Document Reproduction Service No. ED 038 350.

Washington School of Psychiatry. "Teacher Corps—Two Years of Progress and Plans for the Future." October 1968. ERIC Document Reproduction Service No. ED 029 854.

Waterman, Floyd T. "Characteristics of Competency Based Teacher Education Programs." In *Competency Based Teacher Education: A Potpourri of Perspectives*. Washington, DC: Association of Teacher Education, 1974.

Weiner, Lois. "Cracks in Shanker's Empire." *New Politics* 11 (Fall 1976): 51–57.

Weiner, Lois. "Death Wish among the Teachers." *The Nation* 24, September 1977, 276–277.

Weiner, Lois. "Captive Voices—Are They Still?" *Communication: Journalism Education Today* 12 (Spring 1979): 4–6.

Weiner, Lois. "Warning: Textbooks Are Not Made or Used in Heaven." *English Journal* (December 1979): 7–10.

Weiner, Lois. "Democratizing the Schools." *New Politics* 1 (Summer 1987): 81–94.

Weiner, Lois. "Policy Makers Take Note: The Motivations of Academically Successful Liberal Arts Graduates for Choosing Teaching as a Career." *High School Journal* 73 (October 1989): 1–8.

Weiner, Lois. "Lost at the Crossroads." Paper presented at the annual meeting of the American Educational Research Association, Chicago, April 1990.

Weiner, Lois. "The Corporate Ethos and Educational Reforms." Paper presented at the New England Educational Research Organization, Rockport, ME, May 1990.

Weiner, Lois. "Preparing the Brightest for Urban Schools." *Urban Education* 25 (October 1990): 258–273.

Weis, Lois, Eleanor Farrar, and Hugh C. Petrie, eds. *Dropouts from School: Issues, Dilemmas, and Solutions*. Albany: State Univ. of New York Press, 1989.

Weiss, Samuel. "CUNY and School Chancellors to Confer on Goals." *New York Times*, 5 June 1990, p. B3.

Welker, Robert. *The Teacher as Expert: A Theoretical and Historical Examination*. Albany: State Univ. of New York Press, 1992.

West, Earle H. Editorial. *The Journal of Negro Education* 42 (Summer 1973): 231–232.

White, Louise R. "Effective Teachers for Inner City Schools." *The Journal of Negro Education* 42 (Summer 1973): 308–314.

Wilson, Lucy L. W. *The New Schools of New Russia*. New York: Vanguard Press, 1928.

Wise, Arthur, Linda Darling-Hammond, and Barnett Berry. *Effective Teacher Selection from Recruitment to Retention*. Santa Monica, CA: Rand Corp., 1987.

Wolf, Alison. "The State of Urban Schools." *Urban Education* 13 (July 1978): 179–194.

Wright, Rob. "1994 Target Date Eyed for US Teacher Exam." *The Boston Globe*, 4 September 1988.

Wrigley, Julia. *Class Politics and Public Schools*. New Brunswick, NJ: Rutgers Univ. Press, 1982.

Yeakey, Carol Camp, and Gladys Styles Johnston. "High School Reform: A Critique and a Broader Construct of Social Reality." *Education and Urban Society* 17 (February 1985): 157–170.

Zeichner, Kenneth M. "Contradictions and Tensions in Professionalization of Teaching and the Democratization of Schools." *Teachers College Record* 92 (Spring 1991): 363–379.

Zeluck, Stephen. "The U.F.T. Strike: Will It Destroy the A.F.T.?" *Phi Delta Kappan* 50 (January 1969): 250–254.

Zerchykov, Ross, ed. *A Citizen's Notebook for Effective Schools.* Boston: Institute for Responsive Education, 1986.

Zimpher, Nancy L. "The RATE Project: A Profile of Teacher Education Students." *Journal of Teacher Education* 40 (November–December 1989): 27–30.

Index

About the Author

Lois Weiner completed her undergraduate education at the University of California, Berkeley, and the University of Stockholm, Sweden; her M.A. from Columbia University, Teachers College; and an Ed.D. from Harvard Graduate School of Education. After teaching home economics, journalism, and English in California, she moved to Manhattan, where she has lived since 1978. As a New York City English teacher and union activist, she was involved in several initiatives to redesign the three schools in which she worked. Currently an Assistant Professor of Administration, Curriculum, and Instruction at Jersey City State College, she is involved in teacher preparation and has begun work on a book analyzing the uses and limitations of educational research in urban school reform. Outside of school, she enjoys cooking, swimming, and summers in France with her husband, Michael and daughter, Petra.